THE VEGETARIAN COOK BOOK

Four hundred practical recipes for day-to-day use throughout the year, covering a wide range of delicious and healthy vegetarian and wholefood meals.

THE VEGETARIAN COOK BOOK

400 Delicious Recipes from Starters to Sweets
DOREEN KEIGHLEY

THORSONS PUBLISHERS LIMITED
Wellingborough, Northamptonshire

Produced in co-operation with
The Vegetarian Society of the United Kingdom Ltd.
Parkdale, Dunham Road, Altrincham, Cheshire

First published August 1985
Second Impression November 1985
Third Impression February 1986
Fourth Impression July 1986

British Library Cataloguing in Publication Data

Keighley, Doreen
   The vegetarian cookbook: 400 delicious
   recipes from starters to sweets.
   1. Vegetarian cookery
   I. Title   II. Vegetarian Society (UK)
   641.5'636   TX837

   ISBN 0-7225-1203-1

Printed and bound in Great Britain

Contents

Introduction

Today there is undoubtedly a growing interest in the vegetarian way of living. More and more it is being proved to be a healthier way of life. Men, women and children turn towards vegetarianism for various reasons — health, humanitarian, ethical, spiritual, etc. The health aspect is probably the most significant reason why many people, young and old, give up the eating of fish, flesh and fowl and adopt the vegetarian diet. It has been proved over and over again that meat and meat products can be left out of the diet with every confidence — there are so very many wholesome foods to take their place.

In compiling this cookbook, I have endeavoured to use only wholefood ingredients. The more one can use these wholesome foods in the meals prepared for the family, the better it will be for everyone's health.

The following are basic for a balanced diet. Firstly, replace refined and denatured foods, like white flour, white sugar, white rice and other pale ghosts of foodstuffs, with wholegrain products, compost-grown whole wheat, brown rice, raw cane sugar, etc. It is also best to avoid artificially coloured and flavoured foods.

The main sources of protein in a vegetarian diet consist of the following: cheese — made with vegetarian rennet, several varieties being available; nuts — almonds, Brazil nuts, hazelnuts, cashew nuts, peanuts, pine kernel nuts and so on; pulses — soya beans, lentils, chick peas, butter beans, haricot beans, dried peas, mung beans, black-eyed beans and red kidney beans are some of the more well known varieties. Dairy products like butter and milk should be kept to a minimum; about 2½ to 3oz (70 to 85g) is all that is necessary each day, more produces too much acid in the body. Only a proportion of some food is protein — soya beans 40 per cent, cheese 25 per cent, etc.

A good salad every day is an excellent rule. This will not consist of a couple of limp lettuce leaves and a slice of vinegar-soaked beetroot, but a good plate of raw and grated vegetables, from tomatoes and celery to carrots and raw Brussels sprouts, watercress, Chinese leaves, lettuce, chicory, cabbage, onion, radishes, cress, cucumber; in fact, anything available, embellished with raisins, dates, pineapple, grated or ground nuts, bean shoots, can be used in a salad. Too much olive oil may delay digestion and pass some nutritive elements too far down the digestive system to be fully effective — it is better to eat a salad without heavy dressings, although lemon juice is excellent. Cider vinegar can also be used as a change from lemon juice.

It is important to cook vegetables carefully and for the shortest time possible in a minimum of liquid. It is better never to use salt in the water when cooking vegetables. Use the residual liquid for soups, stocks and gravies, or even drink it. Provided they are clean and not contaminated with chemicals, potatoes are better baked in their jackets.

Finally it is important that fresh and dried fruits and raw nuts should figure in the diet: aim for a wide variety of foods to provide a healthy and interesting diet.

Many people have a mistaken idea that the preparation of vegetarian meals takes quite a lot of time, but this is not true. Some of the more elaborate savouries may take time in the preparation, but there are many quickly prepared appetizing and nutritious vegetarian recipes. With the many herbs, spices and natural flavourings that are available, there is no limit to the recipes that can be prepared. Try experimenting with different flavourings, with the addition of a little sea salt if desired and freshly ground black pepper. Also, it is a good idea to take a little time in garnishing the prepared savouries when ready to serve. Appearance of the finished recipes is as important as the taste.

Three main meals a day are quite adequate and these should consist of a selection from the following:

Breakfast fruit juice and/or fresh fruit, muesli or wholefood cereal and milk or soya milk, wholemeal toast with butter or vegetable margarine and honey, with a drink — cereal coffee, dandelion coffee or weak tea.

Lunch fruit juice, starter or soup; a large salad with cheese,

Introduction

nuts, egg or a hot or cold vegetarian savoury; fresh fruit or hot or cold sweet, with a cup of cereal or decaffeinated coffee to follow.

Dinner fruit juice, starter or soup; vegetarian savoury, jacket potatoes, lightly cooked vegetables, gravy; hot or cold sweet; cheese and biscuits with a hot drink to follow.

Many vegetarian recipes can successfully be frozen and kept in the freezer for up to about 3 months. When freshly prepared, however, the majority of recipes undoubtedly taste better. But it is very useful to have a supply of various meals in the freezer, ready for quick serving if necessary. Most soups can successfully be frozen, together with many vegetarian savouries, puddings, sweets, bread, scones and large and small cakes. When using the frozen foods, thaw them out for a few hours at room temperature and then cook in the oven until heated through. Alternatively, it is often possible to put the frozen foods into an oven and cook until ready to serve — a microwave oven can be used if desired.

A comprehensive list of vegetarian and vegan products is published by The Vegetarian Society in its International Vegetarian Handbook. Copies of the handbook may be obtained from the offices of the Society or from health food stores.

The quantities given in the recipes for starters, soups, savouries, salads and hot and cold sweets are sufficient for six people.

1

STARTERS AND SOUPS

STARTERS

There is a very large number of appetizing vegetarian starters. Hors d'oeuvres are still very popular and many different combinations of salads and vegetarian savouries can be served. Small salads make an excellent first course or alternatively, chilled tomato or fruit juice or sliced melon, etc. Following are a few additional ideas for the first course. In all cases prepare the starter just before serving the meal, perhaps with the exception of pâté recipes, which can be frozen when made and kept in the freezer in a container for 2 to 3 months. When required for use, defrost at room temperature for 1 to 2 hours.

Avocado mousse

2 avocado pears	¼ teaspoon paprika
4 oz (115g) low-fat cream	pepper
cheese	2 egg whites
1 lemon	Slices of tomato
Sea salt	

1 Cut the avocado pears in half, remove the stones and scrape all the flesh out into a mixing bowl.
2 Add the low-fat cream cheese, a little grated lemon rind and juice, together with the sea salt and paprika pepper. Half a teaspoonful of dried mint can be added if desired.
3 Beat the egg whites until quite stiff and carefully fold into the mixture.
4 Place into individual glasses and garnish with slices of tomato.

Avocado salad

3 avocado pears	Lettuce leaves
4 oz (115g) cottage cheese	Cress
1 lemon	

1 Cut the avocado pears in half and remove the stones.
2 Grate a little of the lemon rind and add to the cottage cheese.
3 Place the pear halves on lettuce leaves and fill the centres with the cottage cheese.
4 Pour the lemon juice over the pears and garnish with some cress.

Aubergine fritters

4 oz (115g) wholemeal	Sea salt
flour	1-2 aubergines
1 egg	corn oil
¼ pint (140ml) milk	
1 oz (30g) Parmesan	
cheese	

1 Make the batter either by blending the flour, egg, milk, cheese and sea salt together in a liquidizer until a very smooth mixture is obtained, or use an egg whisk.
2 Allow to stand for 1 hour in a cool place.
3 Peel the aubergines and cut into thin slices.
4 Coat well with the batter and deep fry in hot corn oil until golden brown; drain well and serve immediately.

Variation: In place of aubergines, use thin slices of potato or marrow to make potato or marrow fritters.

Stuffed mushrooms

12 large mushrooms
1 onion
2 tablespoons corn oil
3 oz (85g) grated cheese
2 oz (55g) wholemeal
   breadcrumbs

½ teaspoon sage
sea salt
freshly ground black
   pepper

1 Clean the mushrooms, preferably with a damp cloth.
2 Peel and finely chop the onion and cook in the corn oil for 5 minutes.
3 Remove the stalks from the mushrooms, cut into small pieces and add to the cooking onion and cook for a further 10 minutes.
4 Remove from the heat and add the remaining ingredients.
5 Divide the mixture between the 12 mushrooms and place on a baking dish.
6 Bake at 375°F/190°C (Gas Mark 5) for 15-20 minutes. Serve immediately.

Stuffed tomatoes

12 good-sized tomatoes
8 oz (225g) cottage cheese
4 oz (115g) grated cheese
1 oz (30g) chopped
   walnuts
1 teaspoon soya sauce

2 tablespoons chopped
   chives
sea salt and freshly
   ground black pepper
a little chopped parsley

1 Cut the tops off the tomatoes, scoop out the centres with a small spoon and place the tomatoes on a greased baking dish.
2 Mix the cottage cheese, grated cheese, chopped walnuts, soya sauce, chives and seasoning and fill the tomatoes with this mixture.
3 Sprinkle the chopped parsley on top.
4 Bake at 375°F/190°C (Gas Mark 5) for 30 minutes then serve at once.

Nutty rice fries

6 oz (170g) cooked brown
   rice
3 oz (85g) ground
   hazelnuts
2 eggs
2 tablespoons grated onion

1 tablespoon tomato purée
½ teaspoon basil
sea salt
freshly ground black
   pepper

1 Mix all the ingredients well together.
2 Heat a little corn oil in a frying pan and when hot, drop in spoonsful of the mixture.
3 Fry until nicely brown on both sides; drain well and serve.
4 A small tomato salad is excellent served with these fries.

Rice cheese fries

4 oz (115g) grated cheese
6 oz (170g) cooked brown
   rice
2 eggs
1 tablespoon wholemeal
   flour

2 tablespoons grated onion
½ teaspoon coriander
½ teaspoon cumin powder
sea salt
freshly ground black
   pepper

1 Add the grated cheese to the rice.
2 Beat the eggs and add to the rice and cheese, together with the remaining ingredients.
3 Heat a little corn oil in a frying pan and when hot, drop spoonsful of the mixture in.
4 Turn over when just brown on the bottom and when cooked on the second side, lift out and drain well.
5 Serve immediately with a small salad.

Variation: In place of the grated onion, add 2 tablespoonsful tomato purée.

Bean and peanut pâté

8 oz (225g) cooked butter
   beans
2 oz (55g) peanut butter
1 dessertspoon lemon juice

¼ teaspoon paprika
   pepper
sea salt

1 Mash the beans well then add the rest of the ingredients or alternatively liquidize everything together until quite smooth. Freeze at this point if desired.
2 When well mixed, divide into six and make into oblong or round shapes.
3 Serve on a small decorative salad.

Soya bean and Tartex pâté

8 oz (225g) cooked soya
   beans
3oz (85g) Tartex
1 dessertspoon lemon juice

sea salt
freshly ground black
   pepper

1 Mash the beans well and mix with the other ingredients.
2 Form into six round or oblong shapes, or freeze in a container if desired.
3 Serve with a small salad.

SOUPS

Vegetarians are certainly not limited when it comes to making a soup for the first course of a meal, or a really nourishing one to provide a satisfying meal when served with wholemeal toast, biscuits, etc. Soups are excellent to utilize any water in which vegetables have been cooked. I always recommend the vegetables to be cooked without the addition of salt, and suggest that it can be added when they are served if desired.

With the various ingredients available, numerous different soups can be made. It is a good idea to use fresh vegetables as much as possible, falling back on pulses and cereals during the winter months when the supply of fresh vegetables is limited.

An electric liquidizer is an invaluable aid when it comes to preparing soups. It saves hours of time in sieving, and also ensures that there is no residue, hence all the goodness from the ingredients used goes into the soup.

There are various ways of thickening soups and potatoes are excellent for this purpose. Flour is often used for thickening, but other ingredients can be used such as fine oatmeal, corn meal, rice flour, barley flour, etc. *Emsoy, Vesop* and yeast extracts give added flavour and nutrients, e.g. *Barmene Marmite, Yex, Yeastrel* and *Vecon.*

Soups can be successfully frozen and kept in the freezer. When making soups to freeze, use only sufficient liquid to allow the soup to be liquidized, and add the extra liquid when heating it up. Store the soup in containers and it will keep for 2 to 3 months. Thaw at room temperature and then heat the soup with added liquid and serve. When milk is one of the ingredients of the soup, add this to the soup when it is nearly ready to serve.

Barley cream soup

1 large onion	freshly ground black
1 large carrot	pepper
4 celery sticks	4 oz (115g) pot barley
1 tablespoon corn oil	½ pint (285ml) milk
3 pints (1.7 litres) vegetable	(optional)
stock	2 tablespoons finely
1 teaspoon yeast extract	chopped fresh parsley
1 teaspoon sea salt	

1 Peel the onions and cut into small pieces; cut the carrot and celery into small pieces.
2 Heat the corn oil in a large pan and add the onions, carrot and celery and cook for 10 minutes.
3 Add the vegetable stock, yeast extract and seasoning and the barley and cook over a low heat until the barley is soft — about 2 hours.
4 Rub through a sieve, or use a liquidizer and return to the pan and add seasoning to taste. Freeze at this point if desired.
5 Add the milk (if used) and serve when hot, garnished with parsley.

Note: This soup can also be served as a broth if it is not sieved or liquidized.

Bean soup

6 oz (170g) haricot or	1 teaspoon mixed herbs
butter beans	1 good teaspoon yeast
1 large onion	extract
1 tablespoon corn oil	sea salt
8 oz (225g) tomatoes	freshly ground black
3 pints (1.7 litres) vegetable	pepper
stock	

1 Soak the beans overnight; drain the water off.
2 Peel and chop the onion finely and cook in the corn oil for 10 minutes.
3 Add the chopped tomatoes, vegetable stock and beans and cook over a low heat until the beans are tender; add the mixed herbs.
4 Rub through a sieve, or liquidize, and return to the pan.
5 Add the yeast extract, sea salt and pepper to taste. Freeze at this point if desired, or heat and serve.

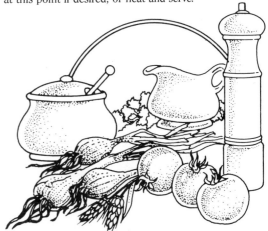

Beetroot soup

1 large onion	1 oz (30g) wholemeal flour
3 sticks celery	½ pint (285ml) milk
1 tablespoon corn oil	1 teaspoon mixed herbs
2 large cooked beetroots	1 teaspoon yeast extract
2 pints (1.13 litres)	seasoning
vegetable stock	

1 Peel and chop the onion into small pieces; wash the celery and cut into small pieces. Cook the onion and celery in the corn oil for 15 minutes.
2 Peel the cooked beetroot and cut into pieces and add, together with the vegetable stock and cook for about 1 hour.
3 Rub through a sieve, or liquidize and return to the pan or freeze at this point if desired.
4 Mix the flour with a little milk and add when the soup is hot, stirring until it thickens.
5 Add finely chopped herbs, yeast extract and seasoning to taste.

Starters and Soups

Chick pea and vegetable soup

6 oz (170g) chick peas
2 onions
2 tablespoons corn oil
1 clove garlic
1 medium sized carrot
3 sticks celery
3 pints (1.7 litres) vegetable
   stock

1 teaspoon marjoram
1 teaspoon sweet basil
1 teaspoon yeast extract
sea salt
freshly ground black
   pepper

1 Soak the peas overnight.
2 Peel the onion, cut into small pieces and cook in the corn oil with the crushed garlic, and the carrot and celery cut into small pieces, for 15 minutes.
3 Add the vegetable stock and chick peas and marjoram and basil and cook until all the vegetables are tender.
4 Add the yeast extract, salt and pepper.
5 The soup can be served with the vegetable pieces whole, or it can be liquidized.
6 Freeze at this point if desired. This soup will keep for about 1 month. Defrost at room temperature and heat the soup up. A microwave oven can be used at this point.

Cream of celery soup

8 celery sticks
1 large onion
2 tablespoons corn oil
1 pint (570ml) vegetable
   stock

2 oz (55g) wholemeal flour
1 pint (570ml) milk
seasoning to taste

1 Wash the celery and cut into small pieces; peel the onion and cut into small pieces, and cook in a pan with the corn oil for 15 minutes.
2 Add the vegetable stock and cook until the celery and onion are tender. Rub through a sieve, or liquidize and return to the pan, or cool and place in a container and freeze at this stage. To use from frozen, defrost at room temperature and complete the soup.
3 Mix the flour with a little milk and heat the remaining milk and add to the soup with the flour and milk. Stir until the soup thickens. Add seasoning to taste.

Leek and lentil soup

6 oz (170g) red lentils
3 pints (1.7 litres) vegetable
   stock
6 leeks
1 dessertspoon yeast
   extract

sea salt
freshly ground black
   pepper

1 Wash the lentils and place in a pan with the vegetable stock and the leeks — washed and chopped (if large leeks are used, four may be sufficient).
2 When the lentils and leeks are tender, rub through a sieve, or liquidize and return to the pan. Freeze at this point if desired.
3 Add the yeast extract, sea salt and black pepper, together with additional vegetable stock, if required.

Leek and potato soup

6 leeks
2 tablespoons corn oil
4 medium-sized potatoes
3 pints (1.7 litres) vegetable
   stock
1 teaspoon dried sage

1 good teaspoon yeast
   extract
sea salt
freshly ground black
   pepper

1 Wash the leeks, cut into small pieces and cook in the corn oil for 15 minutes.
2 Scrub the potatoes and cut into small pieces and add to the leeks together with the vegetable stock. Cook until the leeks and potatoes are tender.
3 Rub through a sieve or liquidize and return to the pan. Freeze at this stage if desired, and when required, thaw at room temperature.
4 Add the sage, yeast extract, sea salt and black pepper and heat the soup, adding extra vegetable stock if necessary.

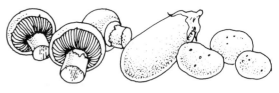

Savoury lentil soup

2 onions
2 tablespoons corn oil
3 pints (1.7 litres) vegetable
   stock
8 oz (225g) red lentils

chopped fresh or dried
   sage
1 good teaspoon yeast
   extract
seasoning

1 Peel the onions, cut into small pieces and cook in the corn oil for 10 minutes.
2 Add the vegetable stock and well-washed lentils and cook over a low heat until tender, adding the chopped sage towards the end of the cooking.
3 Rub through a sieve, or liquidize and return to the pan, or freeze at this stage if desired and thaw at room temperature when required.
4 Add the yeast extract and seasoning to taste, together with extra vegetable stock if necessary.

Mushroom and chick pea soup

8 oz (225g) chick peas
2 pints (1.13 litres)
    vegetable stock
8 oz (225g) mushrooms
2 tablespoons corn oil

1 teaspoon mixed herbs
sea salt
freshly ground black
    pepper
1 pint (570ml) milk

1 Soak the chick peas overnight, then drain.
2 Place the vegetable stock in a pan and add the chick peas and cook until tender.
3 Wash the mushrooms, or wipe with a damp cloth, cut into small pieces and cook for 10 minutes in the corn oil. Add the mushrooms to the cooked peas, together with the mixed herbs.
4 Rub through a sieve, or liquidize and return to the pan, or freeze at this stage if desired — thaw at room temperature when required.
5 Add the sea salt, black pepper and milk and heat over a low heat.
6 Serve garnished with chopped fresh parsley or mint.

Cream of mushroom soup

1 large onion
2 tablespoons corn oil
8 oz (225g) mushrooms
1 pint (570ml) vegetable
    stock

2 oz (55g) wholemeal flour
1 pint (570ml) milk
seasoning

1 Peel the onion, cut into small pieces and cook in the corn oil for 10 minutes.
2 Wash the mushrooms, or clean by using a damp cloth, cut into small pieces and add to the onion and cook for a further 5 minutes.
3 Add the vegetable stock and cook over a low heat until the onions and mushrooms are tender.
4 Rub through a sieve, or liquidize and return to the pan; freeze at this point, if desired, thawing at room temperature when required.
5 Mix the flour to a smooth paste with a little cold milk and add to the soup, together with the heated milk, stirring until it thickens, adding seasoning to taste.

Creamy mushroom soup

12 oz (340g) mushrooms
2 oz (55g) butter
2 oz (55g) wholemeal flour
1½ pints (850ml) vegetable
    stock

1 pint (570ml) milk
seasoning
chopped fresh parsley

1 Wash the mushrooms, or wipe with a damp cloth, and cut into small pieces. Cook in the butter in a pan for 10 minutes.
2 Add the flour and mix well in, then add the warm vegetable stock gradually, stirring well, until all the stock has been added. Freeze at this stage, when the soup is concentrated, if desired and thaw at room temperature when required.
3 Add the warm milk to the thick soup, stirring well, together with seasoning to taste.
4 Sprinkle a little fresh chopped parsley on the soup after serving.

Oatmeal and onion soup

2 onions
2 carrots
2 tablespoons corn oil
2 pints (1.13 litres)
    vegetable stock

4 oz (115g) medium
    oatmeal
yeast extract or soya
    sauce
seasoning

1 Peel and cut the onions and carrots into small pieces and cook in the corn oil for 15 minutes in a pan.
2 Add the vegetable stock and oatmeal and cook over a low heat for about 30 minutes.
3 Rub through a sieve, or liquidize and return to the pan, or alternatively freeze in a container at this stage and when required, thaw at room temperature.
4 Heat in the pan, adding yeast extract or soya sauce and seasoning to taste.

Onion and carrot soup

2 onions
8 oz (225g) carrots
2 tablespoons corn oil
2 pints (1.13 litres)
    vegetable stock

1 dessertspoon yeast
    extract
seasoning

1 Peel and cut the onions and carrots into small pieces and cook in a pan in the corn oil over a low heat for 15 minutes.
2 Add the vegetable stock and cook until the carrots and onions are soft.
3 Rub through a sieve, or liquidize and return to the pan; freeze when cool at this stage if desired and thaw at room temperature when required.
4 Add the yeast extract and seasoning to taste.
5 A little warm milk can be added to this soup just before serving.

Starters and Soups

Onion soup

3 onions
2 tablespoons corn oil
6 oz (170g) potatoes
3 pints (1.7 litres) vegetable
stock

1 teaspoon yeast extract
½ teaspoon coriander
sea salt
freshly ground black
pepper

1 Peel the onions, cut into small pieces and cook in the corn oil over a low heat for 20 minutes.
2 Add the scrubbed and diced potatoes, together with the vegetable stock and cook over a low heat until the onions and potatoes are tender.
3 Rub through a sieve, or liquidize and return to the pan.
4 Add the yeast extract, coriander, sea salt and black pepper.
5 Serve hot with a little fresh chopped parsley — this soup is best made fresh so do not freeze.

Variation:
1 Use two-thirds vegetable stock and one-third milk for the liquid, adding the milk after the soup has been liquidized.
2 Serve with a good sprinkling of grated cheese on each bowl of soup.

Pea and mint soup

8 oz (225g) dried peas
1 large onion
1 tablespoon corn oil
3 pints (1.7 litres) vegetable
stock

1 tablespoon dried mint
1 teaspoon yeast extract
sea salt
freshly ground black
pepper

1 Soak the dried peas overnight; drain off the water.
2 Peel the onion, cut into small pieces and cook in the corn oil in a large pan for 15 minutes.
3 Add the vegetable stock and soaked peas and cook over a low heat until the peas are soft, adding the dried mint. (Fresh mint can be used, in which case, 2 tablespoonsful chopped mint would be required.)
4 Rub through a sieve, or liquidize and return to the pan, or cool and freeze at this stage, thawing at room temperature when required.
5 Heat the soup, adding the yeast extract, sea salt and black pepper to taste, together with the extra vegetable stock if the soup is too thick.

Tomato and rice soup

2 oz (55g) brown rice
2 pints (1.13 lires)
vegetable stock
1 lb (455g) tomatoes

1 oz (30g) butter
½ pint (285ml) milk
seasoning
grated cheese

1 Wash the rice and cook in the vegetable stock until soft.
2 Cut the tomatoes into small pieces and cook in the butter for 5 minutes and add to the cooked rice.
3 Rub through a sieve, or liquidize and return to the pan, or cool and freeze at this stage, thawing at room temperature when required.
4 Add the milk and seasoning to taste.
5 When serving, sprinkle grated cheese on each plate of soup.

Quick vegetable soup

2 onions
2 sticks celery
2 carrots
2 medium-sized potatoes
3 pints (1.7 litres) vegetable
stock
1 teaspoon mixed herbs

½ teaspoon basil
½ teaspoon marjoram
1 teaspoon yeast extract
sea salt
freshly ground black
pepper

1 Peel the onions and cut into small pieces; cut the celery into small pieces; scrub the carrots and potatoes and cut into small pieces.
2 Place all the vegetables in a large pan with the vegetable stock and cook for 10 to 15 minutes, together with the various herbs.
3 Rub through a sieve, or liquidize and return to the pan, or freeze at this stage if desired, having used less vegetable stock for cooking the vegetables. Thaw at room temperature when required and heat in a pan.
4 Add the yeast extract and seasoning to taste. (When using *Marmite*, you do not need to add much extra sea salt.) Other vegetables can also be used in this soup.

Vegetable soup

2 onions
2 tablespoons corn oil
4 oz (115g) carrots
4 celery sticks
1 medium-sized potato
3 pints (1.7 litres) vegetable
stock

1 dessertspoon yeast
extract
1 teaspoon mixed herbs
sea salt
freshly ground black
pepper

1 Peel the onions, cut into small pieces and cook in the corn oil for 15 minutes, together with the carrots and celery cut into small pieces.
2 Add the potato, scrubbed and cut into small pieces, together with the vegetable stock and cook over a low heat until the vegetables are soft.
3 Sieve or liquidize and return to the pan or cool and freeze at this point in a container and thaw at room temperature when required, then heat.
4 Add the yeast extract, mixed herbs, sea salt and black pepper to taste and serve the soup when hot, with a little fresh chopped parsley sprinkled on the top of each plate.

2.

SAVOURIES AND SAUCES

SAVOURIES

In compiling the recipes in this cookbook, I have included many more savouries to serve as the main cooked meal or main salad meal, because it is these recipes that so successfully replace the meat or fish. In fact, it is far easier for a vegetarian cook to plan the daily meals, because the main ingredients like pulses, rice, cereals, nuts, soya proteins, etc. can be kept for quite long periods and are therefore usually in the store cupboard. Many delicious savouries can also be made using cheese and eggs. All savouries should be served either with a large decorative salad, or lightly cooked vegetables, jacket potatoes, savoury sauce, etc. taking particular care regarding the presentation of the various dishes.

In many cases the savouries can, if required, be successfully frozen and kept in the freezer for future use. Two to three months is the length of time recommended to store the savouries, and when they are required, defrost for 1 to 2 hours at room temperature and then cook either in the oven, or a microwave oven, or heat in a pan on a low heat, if the savoury has been made that way.

Barley and onion roast

3 oz (85g) pot barley	1 teaspoon yeast extract
1 pint (570ml) water	1 teaspoon sage
2 medium-sized onions	seasoning
2 tablespoons corn oil	1 egg
4 oz (115g) grated cheese	

1 Soak the pot barley overnight; drain and add fresh water and cook until tender — about 1 to 1½ hours.
2 Peel the onions, cut into small pieces and cook in the corn oil over a low heat for 30 minutes.
3 Drain any surplus water from the barley and add to the onions, together with the remaining ingredients.

4 Place the mixture in a greased baking dish and bake for 30-40 minutes at 375°F/190°C (Gas Mark 5,) until golden brown. When cool, this roast can be frozen for 2-3 months. Defrost at room temperature and heat in the oven for 20 minutes, or up to 10 minutes in a microwave oven.

Cannelloni

1 onion	½ teaspoon paprika
1 tablespoon corn oil	pepper
3 oz (85g) tvp mince	12 sheets wholewheat
¾ pint (425ml) water	lasagne
1 teaspoon yeast extract	14 oz (395g) tin chopped
½ teaspoon basil	tomatoes
½ teaspoon sage	4 oz (115g) grated cheese
sea salt	

1 Peel the onion, cut into small pieces and cook in the corn oil for 10 minutes.
2 Add the tvp mince, water, yeast extract, basil, sage, salt and paprika pepper and simmer for 10 minutes.
3 Cook the sheets of lasagne in boiling water for 5 minutes; drain and separate the sheets.
4 Place the cooled savoury mixture on each lasagne sheet and roll up.
5 Grease a large flat baking dish and place in this half the tomatoes together with seasoning to taste.
6 Place the rolled lasagne sheets on the tomatoes and cover with the remaining tomatoes, seasoned to taste.
7 Cover the top with grated cheese and bake at 400°F/200°C (Gas Mark 6) for 30-40 minutes. The rolled up lasagne sheets can be frozen if desired and kept for 2-3 months, and then the savoury can be made up after defrosting at room temperature, with the tomatoes and the cheese topping.

Savouries and Sauces

Bulgar wheat roast

2 onions
2 tablespoons corn oil
1 red pepper
2 medium sized courgettes
½ pint (285ml) vegetable
  stock
6 oz (170g) bulgar wheat
4 oz (115g) grated cheese
1 egg
½ teaspoon marjoram
½ teaspoon thyme
sea salt
freshly ground black
  pepper

1 Peel the onions, cut into small pieces and place in a pan with the corn oil.
2 De-seed the pepper, cut into small pieces and add to the onion, together with the courgettes, also cut into small pieces and cook for 20 minutes.
3 Add the vegetable stock and bulgar wheat and cook for 30 minutes, adding more stock or water if necessary.
4 Add the remaining ingredients and place in a greased baking dish.
5 Bake at 400°F/200°C (Gas Mark 6) for 30-40 minutes. Serve hot with vegetables, or sliced cold with salad.
6 Alternatively, cool and freeze for up to 2-3 months. Defrost at room temperature and cook for 20 minutes in the oven or up to 10 minutes in a microwave oven.

Bulgar wheat and tomato savoury

2 onions
2 tablespoons corn oil
¾ pint (425ml) vegetable
  stock
8 oz (225g) bulgar wheat
6 oz (170g) grated cheese
1 tablespoon tomato purée
½ teaspoon basil
sea salt
freshly ground black
  pepper

1 Peel the onions, cut into small pieces and cook in the corn oil for 20 minutes.
2 Add the vegetable stock and bulgar wheat and cook over a low heat for 30-40 minutes.
3 Add the remaining ingredients and serve when thoroughly hot. This recipe can be frozen if liked, in which case, omit the cheese and store for 2-3 months. Defrost at room temperature and heat over a low heat in a pan, adding the grated cheese.

Lasagne

1 onion
1 tablespoon corn oil
4 oz (115g) Protoveg
  minced
1 tin (14 oz/395g) tomatoes
  in tomato juice
1 teaspoon mixed herbs
½ teaspoon coriander
½ teaspoon ground cumin
sea salt
freshly ground black
  pepper
12 sheets wholemeal
  lasagne
4 oz (115g) grated cheddar
  cheese

1 Peel the onion, cut into small pieces and cook in the corn oil over a low heat for 15 minutes.
2 Add the minced *Protoveg* — plain or beef flavour, with 3 cupsful water and cook over a low heat for 5 minutes.
3 Add the tomatoes, cut into small pieces and the juice, together with all the seasoning ingredients.
4 Place a thin layer of the cooked mixture into a greased baking dish; cover with 4 sheets of wholewheat lasagne, then a further layer of the cooked mixture and so on.
5 Sprinkle the grated cheese on top and bake at 375°F/190°C (Gas Mark 5) for 30-40 minutes. Freeze if desired, when cool.

Macaroni and tomato bake

6 oz (170g) wholemeal
  macaroni
½ pint (285ml) water
1 tablespoon wholemeal
  flour
¼ pint (140ml) milk
6 oz (170g) grated cheese
1 tablespoon tomato purée
2 eggs
seasoning

1 Cook the macaroni in water until it is *al dente*.
2 Mix the flour with a little cold milk and pour over the macaroni, adding the remainder of the milk (heated) and stir until it thickens.
3 Add the grated cheese, tomato purée, beaten eggs and seasoning.
4 Place the mixture in a greased baking dish and bake for 30-40 minutes at 350°F/180°C (Gas Mark 4). (Not suitable for freezing.)

Macaroni cheese

6 oz (170g) wholemeal macaroni	1 oz (30g) wholemeal flour
2 oz (55g) vegetable margarine	1 pint (570ml) warm milk
	8 oz (225g) grated cheese
	seasoning

1 Cook the macaroni in sufficient water until it is *al dente*.
2 Melt the margarine, add the flour and cook over a low heat for 2 minutes.
3 Gradually add the warm milk to the margarine and flour, stirring well until all the milk has been added.
4 Add half the grated cheese and seasoning to taste.
5 Place in a greased dish and sprinkle the remaining cheese on top.
6 Place under the grill and cook the cheese until golden brown.
7 This savoury can also be cooked in a moderate oven for 30 minutes — 350°F/180°C (Gas Mark 4). Do not freeze — this savoury is best made fresh.

Macaroni onion cheese

3 medium-sized onions	8 oz (225g) grated cheese
½ pint (285ml) water	seasoning
4 oz (115g) wholemeal macaroni	milk

1 Peel the onion, cut into small pieces and cook in the water for 10 minutes.
2 Add the macaroni and cook until the onions and macaroni are just soft, then drain.
3 Add half the grated cheese, seasoning and a little milk and place in a greased baking dish.
4 Sprinkle the remaining cheese on top and bake at 375°F/190°C (Gas Mark 5) for 30 minutes, until the cheese topping is golden brown. Do not freeze.

Macaroni burgers

4 oz (115g) wholemeal macaroni	1 teaspoon sage
4 oz (115g) ground Brazil nuts	⅛ teaspoon nutmeg
4 oz (115g) grated cheese	seasoning
	1 egg

1 Cook the macaroni in just sufficient water until soft; drain well.
2 Add the remaining ingredients and when cool, form into burgers.
3 Deep fry in hot corn oil or vegetable fat until golden brown; drain and serve hot with vegetables, or cold with salad. Do not freeze.

Millet and cheese rissoles

2 onions	1 teaspoon sage
2 tablespoons corn oil	⅛ teaspoon nutmeg
3 oz (85g) millet flakes	seasoning
8 oz (225g) grated cheese	1 egg

1 Peel the onions, cut into small pieces and cook in the corn oil for 15 minutes over a low heat.
2 Add the millet flakes and cook for a further few minutes, adding a little vegetable water if the mixture becomes too stiff.
3 Remove from the heat and add the grated cheese, sage, nutmeg, seasoning and beaten egg.
4 When cool, form into rissoles and fry in corn oil until nicely brown. The rissoles can be dipped in beaten egg and coated with dried breadcrumbs before frying if desired. Do not freeze.

Millet and mushroom pudding

4 oz (115g) mushrooms	¼ pint (140ml) milk
1 oz (30g) butter or vegetable margarine	4 oz (115g) grated cheese
2 oz (55g) millet flakes	seasoning
	2 eggs, separated

1 Wipe the mushrooms with a damp cloth to clean and cut into small pieces. Cook for 5 minutes in the butter or margarine.
2 Add the millet flakes and milk and allow to cook for 5 minutes.
3 Remove from the heat and add the grated cheese, seasoning and egg yolks.
4 Beat the egg white until stiff and carefully fold into the mixture.
5 Place in a greased baking dish and bake at 350°F/180°C (Gas Mark 4) for 30-40 minutes then serve immediately. Do not freeze.

Millet and nut rissoles

2 onions	1 teaspoon yeast extract
2 tablespoons corn oil	1 teaspoon sage
3 oz (85g) millet flakes	seasoning
6 oz (170g) mixed ground nuts (e.g., hazels, Brazils, cashews, etc.)	1 egg

1 Peel the onion, cut into small pieces and cook in the corn oil for 15 minutes over a low heat.
2 Add the millet flakes and cook for 10 minutes.
3 Remove from the heat and add the remaining ingredients.
4 When cool, form into rissoles and if desired, coat in beaten egg and roll in millet flakes.
5 Fry in hot corn oil or vegetable fat until golden brown; drain and serve. Not suitable for freezing.

Savouries and Sauces

Millet and onion savoury

2 onions
2 tablespoons corn oil
8 oz (225g) millet flakes
4 oz (115g) grated cheese
1 teaspoon soya sauce

½ teaspoon basil
½ teaspoon thyme
sea salt
freshly ground black
    pepper

1 Peel the onions, cut into small pieces and cook for 20 minutes in the corn oil over a low heat.
2 Add just under 1½ pints (850ml) cold water and the millet and cook over a low heat for 15 minutes.
3 Add the remaining ingredients, and when the mixture is nice and hot, it is ready to serve. Should it become a little dry, add more water or vegetable stock. This savoury could be frozen and kept in the deep freezer, but it is better made fresh.

Millet and tomato roast

1½ pints (850ml) cold
    water
8 oz (225g) millet flakes
6 oz (170g) grated cheese
2 tablespoons tomato
    purée

2 eggs
¼ pint (140ml) milk
sea salt
freshly ground black
    pepper
½ teaspoon marjoram

1 Place the cold water in a pan with the millet and slowly bring to the boil.
2 Allow to cook over a low heat for about 15 minutes.
3 Add the grated cheese, tomato purée, beaten egg, milk, sea salt, black pepper and marjoram.
4 Place in a greased baking dish and bake at 400°F/200°C (Gas Mark 6) for 30 minutes, until golden brown. Not recommended for freezing.

Mushroom and macaroni cheese

6 oz (170g) wholemeal
    macaroni
2 oz (55g) butter or
    vegetable margarine
4 oz (115g) mushrooms

1 oz (30g) wholemeal flour
½ pint (285ml) milk
6 oz (170g) grated cheese
seasoning

1 Cook the macaroni in just sufficient water until *al dente.*
2 Melt the butter in a pan and add the washed sliced mushrooms and cook for 5 minutes.
3 Add the wholemeal flour to the mushrooms and then gradually add the milk, stirring well.
4 Add half the grated cheese and seasoning and pour the sauce over the macaroni in a greased baking dish.
5 Sprinkle the remaining grated cheese over the top and bake at 375°F/190°C (Gas Mark 5) for 30 minutes.

6 This savoury can be cooked under the grill instead of in the oven and served when the cheese is golden brown. Not recommended for freezing.

Oatmeal and cheese roast

1 large onion
2 tablespoons corn oil
3 oz (85g) fine oatmeal
¼ pint (140ml) vegetable
    stock

4 oz (115g) grated cheese
1 teaspoon yeast extract
½ teaspoon basil
seasoning
1 egg

1 Peel the onion, cut into small pieces and cook for 15 minutes in a pan with the corn oil.
2 Add the oatmeal and vegetable stock and cook over a low heat for a further 15 minutes, stirring from time to time.
3 Remove from the heat and add the remaining ingredients.
4 Bake in a greased baking dish at 375°F/190°C (Gas Mark 5) for about 30 minutes.
5 Cool and freeze if desired, it will keep for 2-3 months. Defrost at room temperature and heat in the oven for 20 minutes — 10 minutes or less in a microwave oven.

Oatmeal soufflé

1 onion
1 tablespoon corn oil
4 oz (115g) fine or medium
    oatmeal
½ pint (285ml) vegetable
    water

6 oz (170g) grated cheese
2 eggs, separated
seasoning

1 Peel the onion, cut into small pieces and cook in the corn oil for 15 minutes.
2 Add the oatmeal and vegetable water and cook over a low heat for 20 minutes stirring from time to time, and adding more water if required.
3 Remove from the heat and add the grated cheese, egg yolks and seasoning.
4 Beat the egg whites until quite stiff and carefully fold into the mixture.
5 Place in a greased soufflé dish and bake 375°F/190°C (Gas Mark 5) for 30-40 minutes. Serve immediately. Do not freeze.

Oat and onion roast

3 onions
2 tablespoons corn oil
4 oz (115g) rolled oats
8 oz (225g) grated cheese

1 teaspoon yeast extract
1 teaspoon mixed herbs
seasoning
2 eggs

1 Peel the onions, cut into small pieces and cook in the corn oil for 15 minutes.
2 Add the rolled oats, grated cheese, yeast extract, mixed herbs, seasoning and beaten eggs and place the mixture in a greased baking dish.
3 Bake at 375°F/190°C (Gas Mark 5) for 30-40 minutes.
4 For a lighter roast, separate the egg yolks and whites and add the stiffly beaten egg whites last, folding in carefully. Do not freeze.

Pasta shell savoury

2 tablespoons corn oil
2 onions
2 cloves garlic
4 sticks celery
14 oz (395g) tin chopped
  tomatoes
8 oz (225g) wholemeal
  pasta shells

½ teaspoon basil
½ teaspoon rosemary
sea salt
freshly ground black
  pepper
6 oz (170g) grated cheese

1 Warm the corn oil in a pan and add the peeled, finely chopped onion, crushed garlic and celery, cut into small pieces, and cook for 15 minutes.
2 Add the chopped tomatoes and pasta shells and just sufficient water to cover.
3 Cook for 10-15 minutes, together with the basil, rosemary, sea salt and black pepper.
4 Lastly add the grated cheese and cook over a low heat until the cheese has melted. This savoury is not really suitable for freezing — it is better served freshly made.

Cheesy pasta shells

12 oz (340g) wholemeal
  pasta shells
2 onions
2 oz (55g) vegetable
  margarine
4 sticks celery
2 oz (55g) wholemeal flour
1 pint (570ml) milk

sea salt
freshly ground black
  pepper
1 teaspoon dry mustard
6 oz (170g) grated cheese
2 oz (55g) wholemeal
  breadcrumbs

1 Cook the pasta shells in sufficient water until *al dente* — drain.
2 Peel the onions, cut into small pieces, and cook in the margarine for 20 minutes together with the finely chopped celery.
3 Add the flour and allow to cook for 1 minute, before gradually adding the milk to make a sauce.
4 Add the salt, pepper, mustard and half the grated cheese; mix in the pasta.
5 Place the mixture in a greased baking dish and sprinkle the remaining cheese on top, mixed with the breadcrumbs.

6 Bake at 375°F/190°C (Gas Mark 5) for about 30 minutes. (Not really suitable for freezing.)

SAUCES

Sauces are an important addition to the main course of the meal, perhaps more so in vegetarian catering. Following are just a few, although there are many different appetizing sauces that can easily be made. As a change from thickening with wholemeal (wholewheat) flour, use rice flour, maize flour or barley flour, and experiment with all the different herbs and spices. With savouries like nut roasts, savoury pastry rolls, rissoles and so on some type of sauce is an excellent addition to the main course, because these savouries can be dry by themselves.

Brown gravy

2oz (55g) butter or
  vegetable margarine
2 oz (55g) wholemeal flour
1 pint (570ml) vegetable
  stock

1 dessertspoon yeast
  extract
seasoning

1 Melt the butter or margarine in a pan and mix in the flour and allow to cook over a low heat for a few minutes, until the butter and flour brown very slightly.
2 Add the vegetable stock gradually, stirring well.
3 Finally add the yeast extract and seasoning to taste.
4 Freeze when cool, if desired. Defrost at room temperature and stir very well when re-heating.

Cheese sauce

2 oz (55g) butter
2 oz (55g) wholemeal flour
1 pint (570ml) milk

paprika pepper
sea salt
6 oz (170g) grated cheese

1 Melt the butter in a saucepan and add the flour, mixing well until a thick roux is formed.
2 Warm the milk and slowly add to the butter and flour, stirring well to make a smooth sauce.
3 Add the pepper and sea salt to taste and lastly add the grated cheese.
4 Keep the sauce warm over a very low heat, or cool and freeze if desired. Defrost at room temperature for 1 to 2 hours and heat gently, stirring very well.

Savouries and Sauces

Mushroom sauce

4 oz (115g) mushrooms	sea salt
2 oz (55g) butter	paprika or freshly ground
1 oz (30g) wholemeal flour	black pepper
½ pint (285ml) milk	

1 Wipe the mushrooms with a damp cloth and cut into small pieces and cook in the butter for 5 minutes.
2 Add the flour and allow to cook for 2 minutes.
3 Gradually add the warmed milk, stirring well, then add seasoning to taste.

Variations:
1 Add 4 oz (115g) grated cheese to make Mushroom and Cheese Sauce.
2 For a thick mushroom sauce to use as filling for savoury pies, use double the quantity of mushrooms and flour.

Note: All these recipes can be frozen when cool and kept in a container in the freezer. Defrost for 1 to 2 hours at room temperature and stir very well when re-heating.

Onion gravy

2 large onions	1 dessertspoon yeast
2 oz (55g) butter or	extract
vegetable margarine	seasoning
1 oz (30g) wholemeal flour	
1 pint (570ml) vegetable	
water	

1 Peel the onions, cut into small pieces and cook in the butter or margarine in a saucepan over a low heat for 30 minutes, until the onions are tender and a little browned if desired.
2 Add the flour and mix well into the cooked onions.
3 Gradually add the hot vegetable water, stirring well, and finally add the yeast extract and seasoning to taste. Do not freeze.

Onion sauce

1 large onion	sea salt
1 oz (30g) butter	freshly ground black
1 oz (30g) wholemeal flour	pepper
½ pint (285ml) milk	

1 Peel the onion, cut into very small pieces and cook in the butter over a low heat for 15 minutes.
2 Add the flour and then gradually add the warmed milk, stirring well.
3 Add seasoning to taste and serve when nearly boiling. Other spices and seasonings can be added, to vary the flavour, and soya milk can be used in place of milk. Do not freeze.

Quick parsley sauce

1 oz (30g) fresh parsley	2 oz (55g) wholemeal flour
a little water	¾ pint (425ml) milk (or
2 oz (55g) butter or	soya or plant milk)
vegetable margarine	seasoning

1 Liquidize the parsley with a little water.
2 Melt the butter or margarine in a saucepan and add the flour, allowing to cook for 2 to 3 minutes.
3 Gradually add the liquidized parsley to the butter and flour mixture, stirring well.
4 Add the warmed milk, stirring, and the seasoning to taste.
5 Cool at this point if freezing, freeze and when required, defrost at room temperature and stir very well when heating up.
6 Bring gently to near boiling and then serve.

Tomato sauce

1 oz (30g) butter	freshly ground black
1 oz (30g) wholemeal flour	pepper
½ pint (285ml) tomato	1 teaspoon flaked or dried
juice	mint
sea salt	

1 Place the butter and flour in a saucepan and cook over a low heat for 1 minute.
2 Gradually add the tomato juice, stirring well.
3 Add the salt, pepper and flaked or dried mint and serve when nearly boiling.
4 Alternatively, cool and freeze in a container, if desired. When required, defrost at room temperature and stir well when heating in a saucepan.

Variation: For Tomato and Cheese Sauce, add 3 oz (85g) grated cheese to the sauce just before serving.

3.

CHEESE AND NUT DISHES

Cheese and Potato Rocks

8 oz (225g) grated cheese
8 oz (225g) cooked
   mashed potatoes
dried wholemeal
   breadcrumbs or 2 oz
   (55g) rissole powder*

½ teaspoon sage
½ teaspoon chopped mint
⅛ teaspoon nutmeg
seasoning
2 egg whites

1 Add the grated cheese to the mashed potato whilst still warm and mix well.
2 Add the rissole powder, sage, chopped mint, nutmeg and seasoning to taste.
3 Beat the egg whites until quite stiff and fold into the mixture.
4 Place spoonfuls on a greased baking sheet and bake at 350°F/180°C (Gas Mark 4) for 15 to 20 minutes. Serve immediately. Not suitable for freezing.
5 Alternatively, the mixture can be formed into rissoles and fried in corn oil, or cooked under the grill, turning over when the top side is brown.
  *For rissole powder, use *Sosmix* or *Rissolnut*, or something similar, in place of dried breadcrumbs should the latter not be readily available.

Cheesy potato rissoles

8 oz (225g) cooked
   mashed potato
8 oz (225g) grated cheese
2 oz (55g) dried
   wholemeal breadcrumbs

½ teaspoon sweet basil
¼ teaspoon coriander
⅛ teaspoon cumin
seasoning
2 eggs

1 Mix all the ingredients well together.
2 Form into rissoles and, if desired, coat with beaten egg and breadcrumbs.

3 Fry in corn oil until golden brown; drain well and serve.
4 Alternatively, bake in a greased baking dish in a hot oven — 375°F/190°C (Gas Mark 5) for about 20 minutes, turning the rissoles over when half cooked. (Not suitable for freezing.)

Cheese and potato savoury

2 onions
2 tablespoons corn oil
1 lb (455g) potatoes
1 large cooking apple
8 oz (225g) grated cheese

sea salt
freshly ground black
  pepper
½ pint (285ml) vegetable
  stock

1 Peel and slice the onions and cook in the corn oil for 15 minutes.
2 Peel and slice the potatoes and apple.
3 Place alternate layers of onion, potatoes, apple, grated cheese and seasoning in greased baking dish, ending with a layer of cheese.
4 Pour the vegetable stock over, adding a little yeast extract if desired.
5 Place a lid or another dish on top, and bake for 45 minutes at 350°F/180°C (Gas Mark 4).
6 Remove the lid or dish and cook for a further 20-30 minutes, until the cheese topping is golden brown. (Not suitable for freezing.)

Cheese and Nut Dishes

Cheese and potato pudding

8 oz (225g) grated cheese
8 oz (225g) cooked
  mashed potato
2 large eggs

¼ pint (140ml) milk
sea salt
freshly ground black
  pepper

1 Add the grated cheese to the warm mashed potato.
2 Beat the eggs with the milk and add to the potato and cheese, together with the salt and pepper.
3 Place in a greased baking dish and bake at 375°F/190°C (Gas Mark 5) for 30 minutes. (Not suitable for freezing.)

Variations:
1 Add 2 tablespoonsful tomato purée to the mixture to make Cheese, Potato and Tomato Pudding.
2 Add 1 onion, peeled, cut into small pieces and cooked in a little corn oil, together with ½ teaspoonful sage and ½ teaspoonful yeast extract to make a Savoury Cheese Pudding.

Cheese puddings

1 egg
4 oz (115g) wholemeal
  flour
½ pint (285ml) milk

4 oz (115g) grated cheese
a little grated onion
seasoning

1 Make a smooth batter with the egg, flour and milk; allow to stand for one hour, then add the grated cheese, a little grated onion and seasoning.
2 Place a little corn oil or vegetable fat in individual baking dishes and place in a hot oven for 2 minutes.
3 Pour the cheese batter in and bake for 10 to 15 minutes in a hot oven 400°F/200°C (Gas Mark 6). (Not suitable for freezing.)

Baked cheese savoury

2 medium sized onions
2 tablespoons corn oil
6 oz (170g) grated cheese

¼ pint milk (140ml)
3 eggs
seasoning

1 Peel and grate the onion and cook in the corn oil for 10 minutes.
2 Add the grated cheese, milk, beaten eggs and seasoning, mixing well.
3 Bake at 350°F/180°C (Gas Mark 4) for 30 minutes, until the savoury is set and golden brown. The baking dish can be placed in a larger dish containing water to enable the savoury to cook better. Do not freeze.

Cheese soufflé

2 oz (55g) butter
2 oz (55g) wholemeal flour
½ pint (285ml) milk
4 oz (115g) grated cheese
sea salt

freshly ground black
  pepper
¼ teaspoon nutmeg
4 eggs

1 Melt the butter in a pan, add the flour and cook the mixture over a low heat for 2 minutes.
2 Add the warmed milk gradually, mixing well, until all the milk has been added.
3 Remove from the heat and add the grated cheese, sea salt, pepper and nutmeg.
4 Separate the egg yolks and whites and add the yolks to the mixture.
5 Beat the egg whites until quite stiff and carefully fold into the mixture.
6 Place in a well-greased soufflé dish and bake at 375°F/190°C (Gas Mark 5) for 30 minutes, until well risen and golden brown. Serve immediately. Do not freeze.

Cheese and tomato pudding

12 oz (340g) tomatoes
1 oz (30g) vegetable
  margarine
2 oz (55g) polenta (maize
  meal)

6 oz (170g) grated cheese
sea salt
freshly ground black
  pepper
2 eggs, separated

1 Skin* the tomatoes, chop and cook in the margarine for 10 minutes. A little grated onion can be added if desired.
2 Add the polenta and cook for 5 minutes, stirring from time to time.
3 Remove from the heat and add the grated cheese, sea salt, black pepper to taste and the egg yolks.
4 Beat the egg whites until quite stiff and fold into the mixture.
5 Place in a greased baking dish and bake for 30 to 40 minutes at 350°F/180°C (Gas Mark 4). Serve immediately. Do not freeze.

* The best way to skin tomatoes is to place them in a bowl, pour over boiling water and leave for 1 minute, then pour over cold water. The skins can then be removed easily.

Savoury cheese rissoles

1 onion
1 tablespoon corn oil
2½ oz (70g) wholemeal
*   flour*
½ pint (285ml) milk
8 oz (225g) grated cheese
2 oz (55g) dried
*   wholemeal breadcrumbs*

½ teaspoon sage or basil
⅛ teaspoon nutmeg
seasoning
beaten egg and wholemeal
*   breadcrumbs*

1 Peel and grate the onion and cook for 10 minutes in the corn oil.
2 Add the flour and cook for 1 minute before gradually adding the warmed milk, stirring well, to make a thick sauce. Remove from the heat when fully thickened.
3 Add the grated cheese, breadcrumbs, sage or basil, nutmeg and seasoning to taste.
4 When cool, form into rissoles and coat in beaten egg and breadcrumbs.
5 Fry in deep hot oil until golden brown; drain well and serve.
6 The rissoles can be baked on a well-greased baking sheet for 15-20 minutes at 350°F/180°C (Gas Mark 4), turning over half way through the cooking. Not suitable for freezing.

Cheese and tomato savoury

1 onion
1 oz (30g) vegetable
*   margarine*
12 oz (340g) tomatoes

6 oz (170g) grated cheese
seasoning
2 eggs

1 Peel and grate the onion finely and cook with the skinned and chopped tomatoes in the margarine for 10 minutes.
2 Remove from the heat and add the grated cheese and seasoning to taste — a grate of fresh nutmeg can be added if desired.
3 Separate the egg yolks and whites and add the yolks to the mixture.
4 Beat the egg whites until stiff and carefully fold in.
5 Place in a greased soufflé dish and bake at 350°F/180°C (Gas Mark 4) for 30 to 40 minutes until risen and lightly brown. Serve immediately. Not suitable for freezing.

Cheese and tomato soufflé

1 lb (455g) tomatoes
2 oz (55g) butter or
*   vegetable margarine*
1 oz (30g) polenta (maize
*   meal)*

8 oz (225g) grated cheese
1 tablespoon tomato purée
seasoning
2 eggs, separated

1 Melt the butter or margarine in a pan and add the skinned and sliced tomatoes and cook for 10 minutes.
2 Stir in the polenta, adding it slowly and mixing well in.
3 Remove from the heat and add the grated cheese, tomato purée, seasoning to taste and the egg yolks.
4 Beat the egg whites until quite stiff and carefully fold in. Place the mixture in a greased baking dish and bake at 350°F/180°C (Gas Mark 4) for 30 to 40 minutes. Serve immediately it is ready. Do not freeze.

Savoury mushrooms au gratin

2 onions
2 tablespoons corn oil
1 lb (455g) mushrooms
2 oz (55g) wholemeal flour

¾ pint (425ml) milk
6 oz (170g) grated cheese
seasoning

1 Peel the onions, cut into small pieces and cook for 10 minutes in the corn oil.
2 Add the washed and sliced mushrooms and cook for a further 5 minutes.
3 Add the flour and allow to cook for a minute or two before gradually adding the warmed milk, stirring well.
4 Add half the grated cheese, and seasoning and place in a greased baking dish, sprinkling the remaining cheese over the top.
5 Bake for 30 minutes at 375°F/190°C (Gas Mark 5), or alternatively, brown the cheese topping under the grill. Cool and freeze this recipe if desired, thawing at room temperature for 1 to 2 hours, before heating in the oven for 20 minutes.

Almond and polenta roast

2 onions
2 tablespoons corn oil
3 oz (85g) polenta (maize
*   meal)*
¼ pint (140ml) water
6 oz (170g) ground
*   almonds*

1 teaspoon yeast extract
1 teaspoon sage
sea salt
freshly ground black
*   pepper*
1 egg

1 Peel the onions, cut into small pieces and cook in the corn oil for 15 minutes over a low heat.
2 Add the polenta and water and cook for 5 minutes, stirring from time to time.
3 Add the remaining ingredients and mix well together.
4 Place the mixture in a greased baking dish and bake for 30 minutes at 400°F/200°C (Gas Mark 6). Freeze when cool, if desired, keeping for 2-3 months. Defrost at room temperature 2-3 hours and bake for 20 minutes in the oven, or up to 10 minutes in a microwave oven.

Cheese and Nut Dishes

Brazil nut and pine kernel roast

3 onions	½ teaspoon sage
3 tablespoons corn oil	1 teaspoon mixed herbs
4 oz (115g) ground Brazil	1 dessertspoon yeast
nuts	extract
4 oz (115g) ground pine	sea salt
kernels	freshly ground black
4 oz (115g) wholemeal	pepper
breadcrumbs	1 egg (optional)

1 Peel the onions, cut into small pieces and cook in the corn oil for 20 minutes.
2 Add the remaining ingredients, adding a beaten egg if desired, and place the mixture in a greased baking dish.
3 Bake at 375°F/190°C (Gas Mark 5) for 30-40 minutes. Cool and freeze if desired; it will keep for 2-3 months. Defrost at room temperature and bake in the oven for about 20 minutes, or a microwave oven for up to 10 minutes.

Note: Cashews or other nuts can be used in place of the pine kernels.

Brazil nut and tomato roast

8 oz (225g) tomatoes	4 oz (115g) fresh
1 oz (30g) vegetable	wholemeal breadcrumbs
margarine	1 egg
4 oz (115g) ground Brazil	1 tablespoon tomato purée
nuts	seasoning

1 Skin and chop the tomatoes and cook for 5 minutes in the margarine.
2 Add the remaining ingredients and place the mixture in a greased baking dish.
3 Bake for 40 minutes at 375°F/190°C (Gas Mark 5). Turn out and garnish with slices of tomato or chopped parsley. Freeze when cold then follow the directions in previous recipe for defrosting, etc.

Chestnut roast

1 lb (445g) chestnuts	1 good teaspoon yeast
2 large onions	extract
2 tablespoons corn oil	1 teaspoon sage
2 oz (55g) dried	seasoning
wholemeal breadcrumbs	1 egg (optional)

1 Slit the chestnuts across with a sharp knife and place on a baking sheet in a hot oven for 15-20 minutes, when the shells should be easy to remove.
2 Cook the shelled chestnuts in just sufficient water until soft; drain and mash them.

3 Peel the onions, cut into small pieces and cook in the corn oil on a low heat for 20 minutes.
4 Add the mashed chestnuts, together with the remaining ingredients and place in a greased baking dish.
5 Bake for 30-40 minutes at 375°F/190°C (Gas Mark 5). Freeze when cool if desired; it will keep for 2-3 months. Defrost at room temperature for 2-3 hours and bake in a hot oven for 20 minutes, or microwave oven for up to 10 minutes.

Chestnut and cheese roast

8 oz (225g) chestnuts	1 egg
2 onions	½ teaspoon sage
2 tablespoons corn oil	⅛ teaspoon nutmeg
4 oz (115g) grated cheese	seasoning

1 Shell the chestnuts and cook in sufficient water until tender; drain.
2 Peel the onions, cut into small pieces and cook for 20 minutes in the corn oil, over a low heat.
3 Mash the chestnuts and add to the cooked onion, together with the remaining ingredients.
4 Place in a greased baking dish and bake for 40 minutes at 375°F/190°C (Gas Mark 5). Serve garnished with chopped parsley. Freeze when cool; keep for 2-3 months and defrost for 2-3 hours at room temperature and bake for 20 minutes in the oven, or up to 10 minutes in a microwave oven.

Chestnut and rice roast

2 oz (55g) brown rice	1 teaspoon yeast extract
8 oz (225g) chestnuts	½ teaspoon mixed herbs
1 large onion	seasoning
1 tablespoon corn oil	1 egg

1 Wash the rice and cook in sufficient water until soft; drain.
2 Cook the shelled chestnuts in water until soft; drain and mash them.
3 Peel the onion, cut into small pieces and cook in the corn oil on a low heat for 15-20 minutes.
4 Add the cooked rice and mashed chestnuts to the onion, together with the remaining ingredients.
5 Place in a greased baking dish and bake at 375°F/190°C (Gas Mark 5) for 30-40 minutes. Serve garnished with chopped parsley, etc. or cool and freeze if desired and defrost, etc. as for Chestnut Roast.

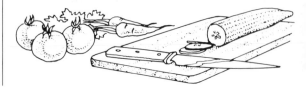

Chestnut pudding

8 oz (225g) chestnuts
1 egg
4 oz (115g) wholemeal
    flour
½ pint milk
seasoning
vegetable cooking fat or
    corn oil

1 Cook the shelled chestnuts in sufficient water until just becoming tender; drain and chop.
2 Make a batter with the beaten egg, flour and milk, adding seasoning to taste. Leave for 1 hour in a cool place.
3 Place the cooking fat or corn oil in a large baking dish and heat for 1-2 minutes in a hot oven.
4 Add the chestnuts to the batter and pour into the baking dish containing the hot fat or oil.
5 Bake at 400°F/200°C (Gas Mark 6) for about 30 minutes, when the pudding should be nicely brown with crisp edges. Serve immediately. Do not freeze.

Chestnut rissoles

8 oz (225g) chestnuts
1 onion
1 tablespoon corn oil
2 oz (55g) dried
    wholemeal breadcrumbs
½ teaspoon marjoram
seasoning
1 egg

1 Shell the chestnuts and cook in sufficient water until soft; drain well and mash them.
2 Peel the onion, cut into small pieces and cook for 15 minutes in the corn oil; add the mashed chestnuts and remaining ingredients and allow to cool.
3 Form into rissoles, dip in beaten egg and breadcrumbs and deep fry in hot cooking oil until golden brown; drain well and serve. It is possible to freeze these rissoles, but they are better fresh.

Chestnut soufflé

8 oz (225g) chestnuts
1 onion
1 tablespoon corn oil
¼ pint (140ml) milk
seasoning
2 eggs

1 Cook the shelled chestnuts in sufficient water until soft; drain and mash them very well.
2 Peel the onion, grate finely and cook for 10 minutes in the corn oil.
3 Add the mashed chestnuts, milk and seasoning to taste.
4 Separate the egg yolks and whites and add the yolks to the mixture.
5 Beat the egg whites until quite stiff and carefully fold into the mixture.

6 Place in a greased soufflé dish and bake in a moderately hot oven 350°F/180°C (Gas Mark 4) for 30 minutes. Serve immediately. Do not freeze.

Hazelnut and walnut roast

3 onions
2 tablespoons corn oil
4 oz (115g) ground
    hazelnuts
4 oz (115g) ground walnuts
4 oz (115g) wholemeal
    breadcrumbs
1 egg
1 teaspoon sage
1 teaspoon yeast extract
seasoning

1 Peel the onions, cut into small pieces and cook in the corn oil for 20 minutes over a low heat.
2 Add the ground nuts, breadcrumbs, beaten egg, sage, yeast extract and seasoning to taste.
3 Place in a greased baking dish and bake at 375°F/190°C (Gas Mark 5) for 30-40 minutes, until brown.
4 Allow to stand for 2 minutes and then turn out on to a warm plate and garnish with slices of tomato and chopped parsley, or freeze when cool and then proceed with defrosting instructions, as for Chestnut Roast.

Light nut roast

2 onions
2 tablespoons corn oil
3 oz (85g) ground
    hazelnuts
3 oz (85g) ground cashew
    nuts
3 oz (85g) dried
    wholemeal breadcrumbs
1 teaspoon yeast extract
1 teaspoon sage
seasoning
2 eggs

1 Peel the onions, cut into small pieces and cook for 15-20 minutes in the corn oil on a low heat.
2 Add the ground nuts, dried breadcrumbs, yeast extract, sage, seasoning and beaten eggs, and place the mixture in a greased baking dish.
3 Bake 375°F/190°C (Gas Mark 5) for 30-40 minutes. Do not freeze.

Cheese and Nut Dishes

Mixed nut roast

2 large onions
2 tablespoons corn oil
4 oz (115g) ground Brazil nuts
2 oz (55g) ground walnuts
2 oz (55g) ground cashew nuts
4 oz (115g) wholemeal breadcrumbs
1 dessertspoon yeast extract
1 teaspoon mixed herbs seasoning
1 egg (optional)

1 Peel the onions, cut into small pieces and cook for 20 minutes in the corn oil over a low heat.
2 Remove from the heat and add the remaining ingredients.
3 Place the mixture in a greased baking dish and bake for 30-40 minutes at 400°F/200°C (Gas Mark 6).
4 Allow to stand for 2 minutes, then turn out and serve suitably garnished. Cool and freeze if desired, storing for 2-3 months. Defrost at room temperature for 2-3 hours and bake for 20 minutes in the oven or up to 10 minutes in a microwave oven.

Stuffed nut roast

For a variation of the above nut roast, use one of the following stuffings; this will then make a roast sufficient to serve about 8 people.

Celery stuffing

1 medium sized head celery
2 oz (55g) vegetable margarine
2 oz (55g) grated cheese
1 teaspoon yeast extract
2 oz (55g) dried wholemeal breadcrumbs
seasoning

1 Wash the celery and cut into small pieces. Cook in the margarine for 20 minutes over a low heat.
2 Add the remaining ingredients and use in the centre of the Nut Roast mixture, baking as for Mixed Nut Roast.

Chestnut stuffing

4 oz (115g) chestnuts
1 onion
1 oz (30g) vegetable margarine
2 oz (55g) dried breadcrumbs
½ teaspoon sage seasoning

1 Remove the shells from the chestnuts by placing them in a hot oven after slitting the skins with a sharp knife. Cook the shelled chestnuts in just sufficient water until tender; then mash well.
2 Peel the onion, cut into small pieces and cook in the margarine for 10 minutes.
3 Mix all the ingredients together.

4 Place the stuffing in the centre of the mixed nut roast mixture and bake the same as for plain Mixed Nut Roast (page 00).
5 The roast can either be served from the dish, or turned out on to a warm plate and garnished with fresh parsley. Freeze if desired.

Stuffed nut loaf

2 large onions
2 tablespoons corn oil
3 oz (85g) ground hazelnuts
3 oz (85g) ground Brazil nuts
3 oz (85g) wholemeal breadcrumbs
1 teaspoon mixed herbs
1 teaspoon yeast extract seasoning
1 egg

1 Peel the onions, cut into small pieces and cook in the corn oil for 15-20 minutes on a low heat.
2 Add the remaining ingredients and mix well.
3 Place half the mixture in a large well-greased loaf tin. Add the stuffing and cover with the remaining nut loaf mixture.
4 Bake at 400°F/200°C (Gas Mark 6) for 30-40 minutes.
5 Turn out on to a warm serving dish and garnish with parsley, slices of tomato, etc. Alternatively, cool and freeze for up to 2-3 months if desired, defrosting at room temperature for 2-3 hours when required and baking for 20 minutes in the oven, or up to 10 minutes in a microwave oven.

Apple and chestnut stuffing

6 oz (170g) chestnuts
1 large cooking apple
1 oz (30g) vegetable margarine
2 oz (55g) wholemeal breadcrumbs
½ teaspoon sage seasoning

1 Skin the chestnuts and cook in sufficient water until soft; drain and mash.
2 Peel the apple, cut into small pieces and place in a pan with the margarine and cook over a low heat until soft.
3 Mix all the ingredients together and use to stuff the nut loaf.

Mushroom stuffing

4 oz (115g) mushrooms
2 oz (55g) butter or vegetable margarine
2 oz (55g) grated cheese
1 teaspoon sage
2 oz (55g) dried wholemeal breadcrumbs
1 tablespoon grated onion
seasoning
1 egg (optional)

1 Wash the mushrooms, or wipe with a damp cloth, and cut into small pieces and cook in the butter or margarine for 5 minutes.
2 Add the remaining ingredients and use as directed.

Tomato and cheese stuffing

6 oz (170g) skinned
  tomatoes
1 tablespoon grated onion
2 oz (55g) butter or
  vegetable margarine

3 oz (85g) grated cheese
2 oz (55g) wholemeal
  breadcrumbs
1 teaspoon chopped mint
seasoning

1 Cook the tomatoes and onion for 5 minutes in the butter or margarine.
2 Add the remaining ingredients and use as directed to fill the Stuffed Nut Loaf.

Onion and nut savoury

3 large onions
2 tablespoons corn oil
4 oz (115g) grated cheese
2 oz (55g) ground
  hazelnuts
3 Shredded Wheat
  biscuits, crushed

2 eggs
¼ pint milk
1 teaspoon mixed herbs
seasoning

1 Peel the onions, cut into small pieces and cook in the corn oil for 15-20 minutes over a low heat.
2 Mix all the remaining ingredients together and use over half to line the bottom and sides of a greased baking dish.
3 Place the cooked onions into the lined dish and cover with the remaining mixture.
4 Bake for 30-40 minutes at 400°F/200°C (Gas Mark 6). Serve immediately the savoury is cooked. Do not freeze.

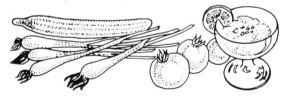

Onion and nut soufflé

2 large onions
2 tablespoons corn oil
4 oz (115g) ground cashew
  nuts
2 oz (55g) dried
  wholemeal breadcrumbs

1 teaspoon yeast extract
1 teaspoon mixed herbs
seasoning
2 eggs, separated

1 Peel and grate the onions and cook for a few minutes in the corn oil.
2 Add the ground cashew nuts, breadcrumbs, yeast extract, mixed herbs, seasoning and the egg yolks and mix well.
3 Beat the egg whites until quite stiff and carefully fold into the mixture and pour into a greased soufflé dish.
4 Bake at 350°F/180°C (Gas Mark 4) for 30-40 minutes, until nicely risen and golden brown. Serve immediately. Do not freeze.

Savoury walnut cutlets

1 onion
1 tablespoon corn oil
12 oz (340g) cooked
  potatoes, mashed
4 oz (115g) ground walnuts
2 oz (55g) ground cashew
  nuts

1 teaspoon yeast extract
1 teaspoon mixed herbs
seasoning
1 egg
a few breadcrumbs

1 Peel the onion, chop finely and cook in the corn oil for 15 minutes over a low heat.
2 Add the remaining ingredients and mix well together. If the mixture is a little soft, add a few dried breadcrumbs.
3 Form into cutlets, coating in beaten egg and breadcrumbs if desired.
4 Fry in hot corn oil or vegetable fat until golden brown. Drain and serve. These cutlets are best made fresh, although they can be frozen if necessary.

4

PULSES AND RICE

PULSES

A great variety of delicious vegetarian savouries can be made using the various pulses that are readily available. It is not necessary to soak red, yellow or green lentils or the mung beans, but the remaining pulses should be soaked overnight — these include chick peas, aduki beans, black-eyed beans, haricot beans, red kidney beans and soya beans. Experiment with all these pulses, together with the many different herbs and spices, and many appetizing savouries, hot or cold, can easily be made. The majority of the pulse savouries can be successfully frozen when cold and kept for 2-3 months in the freezer. Defrost at room temperature for 2-3 hours and then cook for 20 minutes in a hot oven, or up to 10 minutes in a microwave oven.

Bean and cheese savoury

6 oz (170g) haricot beans 1 lemon
3 large onions 1 egg
2 tablespoons corn oil ½ teaspoon mixed herbs
8 oz (225g) grated cheese seasoning
1 good teaspoon yeast
 extract

1 Soak the beans overnight, then drain and cook in sufficient fresh water until tender.
2 Peel the onions, cut into small pieces and cook for 15-20 minutes in the corn oil over a low heat.
3 Add the cooked beans, together with half the grated cheese and the remaining ingredients, including a little grated rind and juice of the lemon.
4 Place in a greased baking dish and sprinkle the remaining grated cheese on top.
5 Bake at 400°F/200°C (Gas Mark 6) for 30 minutes. Serve when the cheese topping is a nice golden brown. This savoury is better made fresh.

Butter bean roast

8 oz (225g) butter beans 1 dessertspoon yeast
3 onions extract
2 tablespoons corn oil 1 teaspoon sage
3 oz (85g) rissole powder seasoning

1 Soak the beans overnight and cook in sufficient water until soft; drain well and mash.
2 Peel the onion, cut into small pieces and cook in the corn oil for 20 minutes over a low heat.
3 Add the remaining ingredients, mixing well together.
4 Place in a greased baking dish and bake for 30-40 minutes at 375°F/190°C (Gas Mark 5). Do not freeze.

Bean and tomato soufflé

4 oz (115g) haricot beans ½ pint (285ml) bean water
2 medium-sized onions or milk
2 tablespoons corn oil 1 teaspoon mixed herbs
2 tablespoons tomato seasoning
 purée 2 eggs, separated

1 Soak the beans overnight and cook in sufficient water until the beans are tender; then drain.
2 Peel the onions, cut into small pieces and cook in the corn oil over a low heat for 15 minutes; allow to cool for a few minutes.
3 Liquidize the beans, onions, tomato purée, bean water or milk, herbs and seasoning, together with the egg yolks.
4 Whisk the egg whites until quite stiff and carefully fold into the liquidized mixture.
5 Place in a greased soufflé dish and bake for 30-40 minutes at 375°F/190°C (Gas Mark 5). Do not freeze.

Haricot bean roast

4 oz (115g) haricot beans
1 large onion
2 tablespoons corn oil
4 oz (115g) grated cheese
1 egg

1 teaspoon yeast extract
½ teaspoon marjoram or
  sage
seasoning

1 Soak the beans overnight and cook in sufficient water until tender; drain.
2 Peel the onion, cut into small pieces and cook in the corn oil for 15 minutes on a low heat.
3 Mash the beans and add to the onion, together with the remaining ingredients.
4 Place the mixture in a greased baking dish and bake for 30-40 minutes at 375°F/190°C (Gas Mark 5). Cool and freeze if desired, and defrost, etc. as instructed in the paragraph at the beginning of this section.

Lentil and hazelnut mould

4 oz (115g) lentils
3 oz (85g) ground
  hazelnuts
3 oz (85g) rissole powder

1 egg
2 teaspoons chopped mint
1 teaspoon yeast extract
seasoning

1 Wash the lentils and cook in sufficient water until soft; drain.
2 Add the ground hazelnuts, rissole powder, beaten egg, fresh chopped mint (use 1 teaspoonful dried mint if fresh mint is not available), seasoning and mix well.
3 Place in a greased pudding basin, cover the top with cooking foil and steam for 2½ hours.
4 Allow to cool for 2 minutes before turning out on to a plate. Decorate with fresh mint. Do not freeze.

Baked lentil roast

8 oz (225g) red lentils
3 onions
2 tablespoons corn oil
3 oz (85g) wholemeal
  breadcrumbs

1 egg
1 level dessertspoon yeast
  extract
seasoning

1 Wash the lentils and cook in just sufficient water until soft — about 30 minutes.
2 Peel the onions, cut small and cook in the corn oil for 20 minutes.
3 Add the cooked lentils to the onion, together with the remaining ingredients.
4 Place in a greased baking dish and bake at 375°F/190°C (Gas Mark 5) for 30-40 minutes. Freeze when cool, if desired.

Lentil savoury

12 oz (340g) red lentils
3 onions
1 dessertspoon yeast
  extract

1 teaspoon mixed herbs
seasoning
a few wholemeal
  breadcrumbs

1 Wash the lentils. Peel the onions, cut into small pieces and place in a pan with the lentils, together with sufficient water, and cook over a low heat until both are cooked and all the water absorbed.
2 Add the yeast extract, mixed herbs, seasoning to taste, and if necessary, a few breadcrumbs to give the savoury a good consistency for serving.
3 This savoury is better made fresh.

Lentil and nut roast

6 oz (170g) red or green
  lentils
1 large onion
1 tablespoon corn oil
4 oz (115g) mixed ground
  nuts

2 oz (55g) dried
  wholemeal breadcrumbs
½ teaspoon sage
1 teaspoon yeast extract
1 egg
seasoning

1 Wash the lentils and cook in sufficient water until soft.
2 Peel the onions, cut into small pieces and cook in the corn oil over a low heat for 20 minutes.
3 Add the cooked lentils to the onion, together with the remaining ingredients and place the mixture in a greased baking dish.
4 Bake at 375°F/190°C (Gas Mark 5) for 30-40 minutes. Serve hot, or cool and freeze; see instructions in the paragraph at the beginning of this section.

Lentil and rice roast

2 oz (55g) brown rice
4 oz (115g) red lentils
1 large onion
1 tablespoon corn oil
4 oz (115g) ground
  hazelnuts

1 teaspoon yeast extract
½ teaspoon sage
1 egg
seasoning

1 Wash the rice and cook for 30 minutes, then add the washed lentils and cook until they are both just soft; drain.
2 Peel the onion, cut into small pieces and cook for 20 minutes in the corn oil over a low heat.
3 Add the rice and lentils to the onion, together with the remaining ingredients and place the mixture in a greased baking dish.
4 Bake at 375°F/190°C (Gas mark 5) for 30-40 minutes. Freeze when cool if desired; see paragraph at the beginning of this section.

Pulses and Rice

Baked lentil and tomato savoury

8 oz (225g) tomatoes
1 onion
4 oz (115g) red lentils
6 oz (170g) grated cheese

1 egg
½ pint (285ml) milk
seasoning

1 Skin and slice the tomatoes; peel the onion and grate finely; wash the lentils.
2 Place layers of tomato, onion, lentils and grated cheese in a greased baking dish with a lid, seasoning each layer.
3 Beat the egg and milk and pour over; season and sprinkle a final layer of grated cheese on top.
4 Bake in a hot oven 400°F/200°C (Gas Mark 6) with the lid on for 45 minutes. Then remove the lid and cook for a further 20-30 minutes until the cheese topping is nicely brown. This savoury is best made fresh.

Lentil cheese roast

8 oz (225g) lentils
1 large onion
1 tablespoon corn oil

4 oz (115g) grated cheese
1 teaspoon mixed herbs
1 egg
seasoning

1 Wash the lentils and cook in sufficient water until tender and all the water has been absorbed.
2 Peel the onion, cut into small pieces and cook for 20 minutes in the corn oil on a low heat.
3 Add the cooked lentils to the onion, together with the remaining ingredients.
4 Place in a greased baking dish and bake for 30-40 minutes at 375°F/190°C (Gas Mark 5). Serve hot, or cool and freeze, if desired.

Lentil onion and cheese bake

2 large onions
2 tablespoons corn oil
8 oz (225g) red lentils
6 oz (170g) grated cheese

½ teaspoon oregano
½ teaspoon basil
seasoning

1 Peel the onions, cut into small pieces and cook in the corn oil over a low heat for 15 minutes.
2 Add the well-washed lentils and sufficient cold water to allow them to cook without becoming too soft.
3 Remove from the heat and add half the grated cheese, oregano, basil and seasoning to taste.
4 Place the mixture in a greased baking dish and sprinkle the remaining cheese on top.
5 Bake in a moderately hot oven 375°F/190°C (Gas Mark 5) for about 30 minutes until the cheese topping is nicely brown. This savoury is best made fresh.

Lentil rissoles

8 oz (225g) lentils
4 oz (115g) ground Brazil nuts
2 oz (55g) dried wholemeal breadcrumbs

1 egg
1 teaspoon yeast extract
½ teaspoon marjoram
seasoning

1 Wash the lentils and cook in just sufficient water until soft.
2 Add the ground Brazil nuts, dried breadcrumbs, beaten egg, yeast extract, marjoram and seasoning to taste.
3 When the mixture is cool, form into rissoles and coat with beaten egg and dried breadcrumbs.
4 Deep fry in hot corn oil until golden brown; drain well and serve. Freeze when cool if desired; defrost at room temperature; and fry, or place frozen rissoles in hot fat and cook until heated through.

Lentil savoury

6 oz (170g) lentils
8 oz (225g) tomatoes
1 tablespoon corn oil
4 oz (115g) ground cashew nuts

3 oz (85g) wholemeal breadcrumbs
1 egg
1 teaspoon yeast extract
1 teaspoon mixed herbs
seasoning

1 Wash the lentils and cook in just sufficient water until soft.
2 Skin the tomatoes by pouring boiling water over them and leaving for 1 minute; cut into pieces and cook in the corn oil for 5 minutes.
3 Add the cooked lentils and the remaining ingredients and place in a greased baking dish.
4 Bake at 375°F/190°C (Gas Mark 5) for about 30 minutes. Freeze at this point if desired; see paragraph at the beginning of this section for defrosting, etc.

Lentil soufflé

6 oz (170g) lentils
1 large onion
1 tablespoon corn oil
seasoning

1 teaspoon yeast extract
½ teaspoon basil
2 eggs, separated

1 Wash the lentils and cook in just sufficient water until soft; sieve or mash them until smooth.
2 Peel and grate the onion and cook for 5 minutes in the corn oil.
3 Add the lentils, seasoning, yeast extract, basil and egg yolks.
4 Beat the egg whites until quite stiff and fold carefully into the mixture.
5 Place in a greased soufflé dish and bake at 350°F/180°C (Gas Mark 4) for 30-40 minutes until well risen and a light brown. Serve immediately. Do not freeze.

Savoury lentil squares

Pastry:
8 oz (225g) vegetable
  margarine
1 lb (455g) wholemeal
  flour
water to mix

Filling:
6 oz (170g) red lentils
2 large onions
2 tablespoons corn oil
1 dessertspoon yeast
  extract
seasoning
1 egg (optional)

1 Make the pastry by rubbing the margarine well into the flour and making into a soft dough with just sufficient cold water (or milk). Leave covered in a cool place until required.
2 Wash the lentils and cook in sufficient water till soft; drain.
3 Peel the onions, cut into small pieces and cook in the corn oil for 20 minutes on a low heat.
4 Add the lentils to the onions, together with the remaining ingredients; allow to cool.
5 Take over half the pastry and roll out to the size of a Swiss roll tin and line with the pastry.
6 Place the filling over the pastry and cover with the remaining pastry.
7 Prick the top well with a fork and bake in a hot oven 400°F/200°C (Gas Mark 6) for 40 minutes. When serving cut into good-sized squares. Can be served hot or cold. Also freeze when cold and keep in the freezer for 2-3 months. Defrost at room temperature and bake in a hot oven for 20 minutes, or they can be placed direct in the oven from the freezer and baked for longer.

Lentil and walnut rissoles

8 oz (225g) red lentils
4 oz (115g) ground walnuts
3 oz (85g) dried
  wholemeal breadcrumbs
½ teaspoon sage

½ teaspoon mixed herbs
⅛ teaspoon nutmeg
seasoning
1 egg

1 Wash the lentils and cook in sufficient water until soft; drain.
2 Mash the lentils and add the remaining ingredients.
3 When cool, form into rissoles and coat with beaten egg and breadcrumbs.
4 Fry in hot corn oil or vegetable fat until a golden brown; drain and serve hot or cold. Alternatively, freeze and keep in the freezer for 2-3 months. To serve fry straight from the freezer, or thaw at room temperature and then fry the rissoles until heated well through.

Lentil and Brazil nut roast

6 oz (170g) lentils
1 large onion
1 tablespoon corn oil
4 oz (115g) ground Brazil
  nuts
3 oz (85g) wholemeal
  breadcrumbs

1 teaspoon sage
1 teaspoon yeast extract
sea salt
freshly ground black
  pepper

1 Wash the lentils and cook in sufficient water until tender; drain.
2 Peel the onion, cut into small pieces and cook in the corn oil for 20 minutes over a low heat.
3 Add the cooked lentils to the onion together with the remaining ingredients.
4 Place in a greased baking dish and bake for 30-40 minutes at 375°F/190°C (Gas Mark 5). Serve hot with vegetables, or sliced cold with salad. Alternatively, freeze when cool; keeping for 2-3 months. Defrost and proceed as instructed in the paragraph at the beginning of this section.

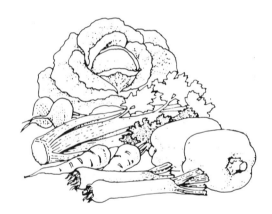

Mung bean savoury

2 large onions
2 tablespoons corn oil
1 pint (570ml) water
12 oz (340g) mung beans
1 dessertspoon soya sauce

sea salt
freshly ground black
  pepper
4 oz (115g) grated cheese
  (optional)

1 Peel the onions, cut into small pieces and cook in the corn oil for 15 minutes on a low heat; a crushed clove of garlic can be added if desired.
2 Add the water and mung beans and cook for 30-40 minutes.
3 Add the remaining ingredients, and when thoroughly hot, it is ready to serve. Should the mixture be a little dry, add more water. Do not freeze.

Pulses and Rice

Onion and chestnut roast

1 lb (455g) chestnuts
3 large onions
2 tablespoons corn oil
3 oz (85g) dried
  wholemeal breadcrumbs
1 dessertspoon yeast
  extract
½ teaspoon sage
sea salt
freshly ground black
  pepper
1 egg (optional)

1 Shell the chestnuts by slitting the skin with a sharp knife and placing in a hot oven for 15-20 minutes.
2 Cook shelled chestnuts in sufficient water to cover until tender; drain and mash.
3 Peel the onions, cut into small pieces and cook in the corn oil for 20 minutes on a low heat.
4 Add the chestnuts, dried breadcrumbs, yeast extract, sage, salt and pepper and the egg, if desired.
5 Place in a greased baking dish and bake at 375°F/190°C (Gas Mark 5) for 30-40 minutes. Serve either hot or cold. (For freezing see the paragraph at the beginning of this section.)

Onion and lentil savoury

3 large onions
2 oz (55g) vegetable
  margarine
12 oz (340g) red lentils
1 dessertspoon yeast
  extract
sea salt
freshly ground black
  pepper

1 Peel the onions, chop finely and cook in the margarine for 15 minutes.
2 Add the washed lentils and sufficient water to cover them; cook until the onions and lentils are tender and all the water has been absorbed.
3 Add the yeast extract, sea salt and black pepper to taste. Serve when hot straight from the pan. Do not freeze.

Savoury bean pie

6 oz (170g) soya beans
2 onions
2 tablespoons corn oil
1½ lbs (680g) potatoes
8 oz (225g) grated cheese
sea salt
freshly ground black
  pepper
¼ pint (140ml) milk
butter or vegetable
  margarine

1 Soak the beans overnight, then pour the water off and cook in sufficient fresh water until tender.
2 Peel the onions, cut into small pieces and cook in the corn oil for 15 minutes.
3 Peel the potatoes and cook in just sufficient water (or steam) until soft.

4 Grease a baking dish and place layers of cooked onion, beans, grated cheese and seasoning, reserving a little grated cheese to add to the potatoes.
5 Mash the potatoes with a little milk, butter or vegetable margarine and the rest of the grated cheese and place on the top, marking with a fork. Freeze at this point if desired; keeping for 2-3 months. Defrost at room temperature and then cook as for the unfrozen dish.
6 Bake for about 30-40 minutes at 400°F/200°C (Gas Mark 6).

Soya bean and cashew nut roast

6 oz (170g) soya beans
2 large onions
2 tablespoons corn oil
4 oz (115g) ground cashew
  nuts
1 dessertspoon yeast
  extract
1 teaspoon mixed herbs
sea salt
freshly ground black
  pepper

1 Soak the beans overnight; drain and cook in sufficient fresh water until soft; drain and mash well.
2 Peel the onions, cut into small pieces and cook in the corn oil for 20 minutes on a low heat.
3 Add the mashed beans to the onions, together with the remaining ingredients.
4 Place in a greased baking dish and bake for 30-40 minutes at 375°F/190°C (Gas Mark 5). Serve either hot or cold. Freeze at this point when cool, if desired, following the instructions in the paragraph at the beginning of this section.

Soya bean soufflé

6 oz (170g) soya beans
1 tablespoon grated onion
4 oz (115g) grated cheese
½ teaspoon coriander
½ teaspoon cumin
sea salt
freshly ground black
  pepper
2 eggs, separated

1 Soak the beans overnight; drain and add sufficient fresh water to cover and cook until tender. Drain excess water off and mash well.
2 Add the grated onion, grated cheese, coriander, cumin, sea salt and black pepper to the mashed beans, together with the egg yolks.
3 Beat the egg whites until quite stiff and fold carefully into the mixture.
4 Place in a greased soufflé dish and bake at 350°F/180°C (Gas Mark 4) for 30-40 minutes until well risen and golden brown. Serve immediately. Do not freeze.

Soya bean and hazelnut cutlets

6 oz (170g) soya beans
4 oz (115g) ground
* hazelnuts*
2 oz (55g) dried
* wholemeal breadcrumbs*
1 teaspoon yeast extract

1 teaspoon sage
sea salt
freshly ground black
* pepper*
1 egg

1 Soak the beans overnight in water; drain and add fresh water and cook until soft. Drain excess water off and mash the beans well.
2 Add the ground hazelnuts, dried breadcrumbs, yeast extract, sage, sea salt, freshly ground black pepper and beaten egg.
3 When cool, form into rissoles and coat with beaten egg and breadcrumbs.
4 Fry in deep corn oil or vegetable fat until golden brown; drain and serve hot or cold. Freeze as for Lentil and Walnut Rissoles.

Baked soya chunks

8 oz (225g) soya chunks
1 pint (570ml) orange juice
2 onions
2 tablespoons corn oil

sea salt
freshly ground black
* pepper*

1 Soak the soya chunks in the orange juice for 1 hour.
2 Peel the onions, cut into small pieces and cook in the corn oil for 15 minutes over a low heat.
3 Add the soaked soya chunks to the onion and cook over a low heat until the soya chunks are soft — alternatively, cook in a covered casserole in the oven, adding the salt and black pepper to taste.

Note: It is better to use flavoured soya chunks in this recipe. Do not freeze. Tomato juice can be used in this recipe in place of the orange juice if preferred.

RICE
Brown rice is a very nutritious food and can be used in many different ways to make appetizing savouries with the addition of nuts, cheese, eggs, vegetables, etc. Brown rice needs more cooking time than the refined white rice but is well worth the extra organization. Most of the rice dishes can be successfully frozen when cold and they can be kept for 2-3 months in the freezer. Defrost at room temperature for 2-3 hours and then cook for 20 minutes in a hot oven or up to 10 minutes in a microwave oven. Alternatively place in the oven straight from the freezer, allowing longer cooking time. Rissoles can be cooked in hot fat straight from the freezer, or allowed to defrost at room temperature and then cooked for a few minutes.

Baked rice curry

4 oz (115g) brown rice
1 onion
1 tablespoon corn oil
4 oz (115g) grated cheese

2 teaspoons curry powder
1 teaspoon mustard
seasoning
2 eggs

1 Wash the rice and cook in sufficient water until soft; drain.
2 Peel the onion, grate finely and cook for 5 minutes in the corn oil.
3 Add the cooked rice to the onion, together with the grated cheese, curry powder, dry mustard, seasoning and beaten eggs.
4 Place the mixture in a greased baking dish and bake for 30-40 minutes at 375°F/190°C (Gas Mark 5). Freeze when cool if desired.

Rice and Brazil nut roast

3 oz (85g) brown rice
1 onion
1 tablespoon corn oil
4 oz (115g) ground Brazil
* nuts*

1 teaspoon yeast extract
½ teaspoon sage
Seasoning
1 egg

1 Wash the rice and cook in sufficient water until soft; drain.
2 Peel the onion, cut into small pieces and cook in the corn oil for 15 minutes.
3 Add the cooked rice to the onion, together with the remaining ingredients.
4 Place the mixture in a greased baking dish and bake at 375°F/190°C (Gas Mark 5) for 30-40 minutes. Serve hot with vegetables or sliced cold with salad. Freeze when cool, if desired.

Rice and nut rissoles

3 oz (85g) brown rice
4 oz (115g) ground cashew
* nuts*
1 teaspoon soya sauce

½ teaspoon basil
seasoning
1 egg

1 Wash the rice and cook in sufficient water until soft.
2 Add the remaining ingredients and, when cool, form into rissoles.
3 Coat in beaten egg and breadcrumbs and fry in hot corn oil until brown; drain and serve hot or cold. Freeze if desired.

Rice and cashew nut soufflé

8 oz (225g) cooked brown
  rice
4 oz (115g) ground cashew
  nuts
2 tablespoons grated onion
2 oz (55g) rissole powder
¼ pint (140ml) vegetable
  stock

½ teaspoon sage
½ teaspoon mixed herbs
1 teaspoon yeast extract
sea salt
freshly ground black
  pepper
3 eggs, separated

1 Mix the rice, cashew nuts, grated onion and rissole powder together.
2 Add the vegetable stock, sage, mixed herbs, yeast extract, sea salt and black pepper, together with the egg yolks.
3 Beat the egg whites until quite stiff and fold into the mixture.
4 Place in a greased soufflé dish and bake at 375°F/190°C (Gas Mark 5) for 30-40 minutes. Serve immediately it is cooked. Do not freeze.

Rice and cheese soufflé

6 oz (170g) grated cheese
8 oz (225g) cooked brown
  rice
2 tablespoons grated onion
1 teaspoon coriander
1 teaspoon cumin

sea salt
freshly ground black
  pepper
2 or 3 eggs, separated
a little milk

1 Add the grated cheese to the cooked rice, together with the grated onion, coriander, cumin, sea salt, black pepper and 2 or 3 egg yolks and mix well together. Add a little milk if the mixture is too stiff.
2 Beat the egg whites until quite stiff and fold into the mixture.
3 Place in a greased soufflé dish and bake at 375°F/190°C (Gas Mark 5) for 30-40 minutes, when the souffle should be well risen and golden brown. Serve immediately. Do not freeze.

Variation:
1 Substitute cooked millet for rice and 2 tablespoons tomato purée for the grated onion to make Millet, Cheese and Tomato Soufflé.

Rice and hazelnut roast

3 oz (85g) brown rice
2 onions
2 tablespoons corn oil
4 oz (115g) ground
  hazelnuts

1 teaspoon yeast extract
½ teaspoon sage
seasoning
2 egg whites

1 Wash the rice and cook in sufficient water until soft.
2 Peel the onions, cut into small pieces and cook in the corn oil for 15 minutes.
3 Add the cooked rice to the onions, together with the ground hazelnuts yeast extract, sage and seasoning.
4 Beat the egg whites until quite stiff and carefully fold into mixture.
5 Place in a greased baking dish and bake at 350°F/180°C (Gas Mark 4) for 30-40 minutes. Serve immediately it is cooked. Do not freeze.

Rice and onion cheese

2 large onions
4 oz (115g) brown rice
1 pint (570ml) water
8 oz (225g) grated cheese

½ teaspoon basil
⅛ teaspoon nutmeg
seasoning

1 Peel the onions, cut into small pieces and cook in the water for 20 minutes.
2 Add the washed rice and cook over a low heat for up to 1 hour, until the rice is tender and the water absorbed into the rice.
3 Add most of the grated cheese, basil, nutmeg, seasoning (sea salt and freshly ground black pepper) and a little milk if the mixture is too stiff.
4 Place the mixture in a greased shallow baking dish and sprinkle the remaining cheese over the top.
5 Bake at 400°F/200°C (Gas Mark 6) for 30 minutes, when the cheese topping should be nicely browned. This savoury could be frozen, but is better made fresh.

Rice cutlets

4 oz (115g) brown rice
1 onion
1 oz (30g) vegetable
  margarine
4 oz (115g) grated cheese

1 teaspoon curry powder
seasoning
2 oz (55g) dried
  wholemeal breadcrumbs
1 egg

1 Wash the rice and cook in sufficient water until soft; drain.
2 Peel the onion, grate and cook for 5 minutes in the margarine.
3 Mix in all the remaining ingredients and allow to cool before forming into cutlets.
4 Coat in beaten egg and breadcrumbs and fry in hot corn oil or vegetable fat until brown; drain and serve hot with vegetables or cold with salad. Alternatively freeze if desired.

Rice and mushroom savoury

8 oz (225g) mushrooms
½ pint (285ml) milk
4 oz (115g) brown rice

1 oz (30g) butter
seasoning
2 eggs

1 Wash the mushrooms, or wipe with a damp cloth, cut into small pieces and simmer in the milk until tender — about 20 minutes.
2 Wash the rice and cook in sufficient water until soft and all the water has been absorbed.
3 Add the rice to the mushrooms, together with the butter, seasoning and beaten eggs.
4 Place in a greased baking dish and bake at 350°F/180°C (Gas Mark 4) for 30-40 minutes. Serve hot. Do not freeze.

Rice, mushroom and cheese bake

4 oz (115g) brown rice	4 oz (115g) grated cheese
4 oz (115g) mushrooms	1 teaspoon curry powder
2 oz (55g) butter or	seasoning
vegetable margarine	1 egg
4 tomatoes	

1 Wash the rice and cook in just sufficient water until soft; drain.
2 Wipe the mushrooms with a damp cloth, cut into pieces and cook in the butter or margarine for 5 minutes.
3 Add the skinned and chopped tomatoes and cook for a minute or two.
4 Add the cooked rice, grated cheese, curry powder, seasoning and beaten egg and place the mixture in a greased baking dish.
5 Bake at 375°F/190°C (Gas Mark 5) for 30 minutes until golden brown. Serve hot, or cool and freeze — see paragraph at the beginning of this section.

Rice and tomato rissoles

4 oz (115g) brown rice	Seasoning
4 oz (115g) grated cheese	1 egg
2 tablespoons tomato	dried wholemeal
purée	breadcrumbs

1 Wash the rice and cook in just sufficient water until soft; drain.
2 Add the grated cheese, tomato purée, seasoning (sea salt and freshly ground black pepper), egg and just sufficient dried breadcrumbs to make the mixture into rissoles.
3 Coat with the beaten egg and breadcrumbs and fry in hot corn oil or vegetable fat until brown; drain and serve. Cool and freeze if desired — see paragraph at the start of this section.

Rice and walnut burgers

4 oz (115g) brown rice	1 teaspoon sage
4 oz (115g) ground walnuts	1 teaspoon yeast extract
2 oz (85g) dried	seasoning
wholemeal breadcrumbs	

1 Wash the rice and cook in just sufficient water until soft; drain well.
2 Add the ground walnuts, dried breadcrumbs, sage, yeast extract and seasoning and when cool, form into burgers.
3 Fry in corn oil until brown; drain and serve, or cool and freeze — see paragraph at the start of this section.

Savoury rice rissoles

4 oz (115g) brown rice	2 oz (55g) breadcrumbs
1 onion	½ teaspoon basil
1 tablespoon corn oil	⅛ teaspoon nutmeg
4 oz (115g) ground	seasoning
hazelnuts	1 egg
4 oz (115g) grated cheese	

1 Wash the rice and cook in just sufficient water until tender; drain.
2 Peel the onion, chop finely and cook for 15 minutes in the corn oil.
3 Add the rice to the onion, together with the remaining ingredients and allow to cool.
4 Form into rissoles and coat in beaten egg and dried breadcrumbs.
5 Fry in hot corn oil until golden brown; drain and serve, or cool and freeze — see paragraph at the beginning of this section.

5

VEGETABLE SAVOURIES

In the main course of a vegetarian meal vegetables form a very important part. They can also be made into many different and very tasty savoury dishes. Following are just a few ideas for appetizing vegetable savouries. Many of the recipes can be frozen and kept in the freezer for up to 3 months. When using them defrost at room temperature and bake for about 20 minutes in the oven, or up to 10 minutes in a microwave oven. It is also possible to put the savouries straight into the oven, which would require more time.

Celery, nut and mushroom savoury

6 sticks celery	2 oz (55g) wholemeal
1 onion	breadcrumbs
2 tablespoons corn oil	1 egg
4 oz (115g) mushrooms	1 teaspoon yeast extract
2 oz (55g) ground walnuts	1 teaspoon mixed herbs
2 oz (55g) ground	seasoning
hazelnuts	

1 Wash the celery, cut into small pieces and cook with the peeled chopped onion in the corn oil for 15 minutes.
2 Add the wiped chopped mushrooms and cook for a further 5 minutes.
3 Add the remaining ingredients and mix well.
4 Place in a greased baking dish and bake for about 30 minutes at 375°F/190°C (Gas Mark 5) until golden brown. Serve hot, or cool and freeze — see paragraph at the start of this section.

Celery and mushroom roast

6 sticks celery	1 egg
2 tablespoons corn oil	1 teaspoon yeast extract
4 oz (115g) mushrooms	1 teaspoon sage
4 oz (115g) grated cheese	seasoning
2 oz (55g) dried	
wholemeal breadcrumbs	

1 Wash the celery, cut into small pieces and cook in the corn oil for 20 minutes over a low heat.
2 Add the chopped mushrooms and cook for a further 10 minutes.
3 Add the remaining ingredients, mix well together and place in a greased baking dish.
4 Bake for about 40 minutes at 375°F/190°C (Gas Mark 5). Serve hot with vegetables, or cool and freeze — see paragraph at the beginning of this section.

Celery and rice roast

1 onion	4 oz (115g) grated cheese
4 sticks celery	1 egg
2 tablespoons corn oil	1 teaspoon curry powder
4 oz (115g) tomatoes	1 teaspoon mixed herbs
2 oz (55g) brown rice	seasoning

1 Peel the onions, cut into small pieces; wash the celery, cut into small pieces and cook both in the corn oil for 15 minutes.
2 Skin the tomatoes and add to the onion and celery.
3 Wash the rice and cook in just sufficient water until soft; drain.
4 Add the rice to the onions, celery and tomatoes, together with the remaining ingredients and place in a greased baking dish.

5 Bake at 375°F/190°C (Gas Mark 5) for 30-40 minutes. Serve as soon as cooked, or cool and freeze — see commencing paragraph to this section.

Stuffed marrow

1 marrow	*2 oz (55g) wholemeal*
2 large onions	*breadcrumbs*
2 tablespoons corn oil	*½ teaspoon basil*
1 medium-sized carrot	*½ teaspoon mixed herbs*
4 oz (115g) ground	*seasoning*
hazelnuts	*1 egg (optional)*

1 Cut the stalk end off the marrow and scoop out the centre. The marrow may be peeled if the skin is hard.
2 Peel the onions, cut into small pieces and cook for 15 minutes in the corn oil. Peel and grate carrot and add, cooking for a further 5 minutes.
3 Add the remaining ingredients and mix well.
4 Place the filling into the marrow and place in a greased baking dish, pressing the top half on well.
5 Bake at 375°F/190°C (Gas Mark 5) for about 40 minutes. Do not freeze.

Marrow au gratin

2 lb (900g) marrow	*½ teaspoon sage*
2 tablespoons corn oil	*sea salt*
2 oz (55g) butter	*freshly ground black*
½ teaspoon coriander	*pepper*
½ teaspoon cumin	*6 oz (170g) grated cheese*

1 Peel the marrow, remove the seeds and cut into small pieces.
2 Heat the oil and butter in a pan and add the pieces of marrow, with the coriander, cumin, sage, sea salt and black pepper and cook over a low heat for 15 minutes.
3 Place the marrow in a baking dish and sprinkle the grated cheese on top.
4 Bake in a hot oven 400°F/200°C (Gas Mark 6) until the cheese is golden brown. Serve immediately with jacket potatoes, vegetables, etc. Do not freeze.

Stuffed marrow slices

1 large marrow	*1 teaspoon sage*
2 onions	*1 teaspoon yeast extract*
2 tablespoons corn oil	*seasoning*
4 oz (115g) ground Brazil	*1 egg*
nuts	*1 large tomato*
4 oz (115g) wholemeal	
breadcrumbs	

1 Peel the onions, cut into small pieces and cook in the corn oil for 15 minutes.
2 Add the Brazil nuts, breadcrumbs, sage, yeast extract, seasoning and beaten egg and mix well.
3 Cut the marrow into 6 slices and scoop out the centres.
4 Place the marrow slices on a greased baking sheet and fill the centres with the savoury mixture, placing a slice of tomato on top.
5 Bake at 375°F/190°C (Gas Mark 5) for about 40 minutes, until the marrow is cooked. Serve hot. Do not freeze.

Marrow, tomato and oat savoury

1 lb (455g) marrow	*1 onion*
4 oz (115g) tomatoes	*1 teaspoon chopped mint*
2 oz (55g) rolled oats	*seasoning*
6 oz (170g) grated cheese	

1 Grease a casserole and place the ingredients in it in layers, commencing with thinly sliced peeled marrow, skinned chopped tomatoes, rolled oats, grated cheese, grated onion, mint and seasoning.
2 Complete until all layers are finished, ending with grated cheese.
3 Place the lid on the casserole and bake for 45 minutes at 375°F/190°C (Gas Mark 5).
4 Remove the lid and bake for a further 20-30 minutes until the cheese topping is golden brown. Serve hot. Do not freeze.

Vegetable Savouries

Moussaka

1 large onion	freshly ground black
1 clove garlic	pepper
2 tablespoons olive oil	8 oz (225g) potatoes
4 oz (115g) tvp mince	2 aubergines
(natural or beef flavour)	1 oz (30g) butter
8 oz (225g) tomatoes	1 oz (30g) wholemeal flour
1 tablespoon tomato purée	½ pint (285ml) milk
1 teaspoon oregano	1 egg
salt	4 oz (115g) grated cheese

1 Peel the onion, cut into small pieces and cook in the oil with the crushed clove of garlic for 5 minutes.
2 Add the tvp mince, skinned chopped tomatoes, tomato purée, oregano, sea salt, black pepper and sufficient water to cook the tvp for a few minutes.
3 Cook the potatoes, peel and cut into small pieces.
4 Slice the aubergines and pour boiling water on them for 1 minute; drain.
5 Arrange layers of tvp mixture, potatoes and aubergines in a greased baking dish.
6 Make a sauce with the remaining ingredients, place the butter in a pan with the flour and gradually adding the milk, stirring until it thickens. Add sea salt and freshly ground black pepper to season.
7 Remove from heat and add the beaten egg and half the grated cheese.
8 Pour the sauce over the tvp, aubergines and potatoes and sprinkle the remaining cheese on top.
9 Bake at 375°F/190°C (Gas Mark 5) for 30-40 minutes. Serve hot. Do not freeze.

Curried mushrooms on rice

8 oz (225g) mushrooms	½ teaspoon turmeric
1 onion	sea salt
2 oz (55g) butter	freshly ground black
1 oz (30g) wholemeal flour	pepper
¼ pint (140ml) milk	1 lb (455g) cooked brown
¼ pint (140ml) vegetable	rice
stock	
1-2 teaspoons curry	
powder	

1 Wipe the mushrooms with a damp cloth and cut into small pieces. Peel the onion, cut into small pieces and cook with the mushrooms in the butter over a low heat for 15 minutes.
2 Add the flour and mix well in, then gradually add the milk and vegetable stock, stirring well.
3 Add the curry powder, turmeric and seasoning.
4 Serve on the cooked brown rice. Not suitable for freezing.

Mushroom rissoles

6 oz (170g) mushrooms	freshly ground black
1 small onion	pepper
2 oz (55g) butter	1 egg
2 oz (55g) wholemeal flour	2 oz (55g) dried
¼ pint (140ml) milk	wholemeal breadcrumbs
sea salt	

1 Cut the mushrooms and peeled onion into small pieces and cook in the butter for 15-20 minutes over a low heat.
2 Add the flour and cook for 2 minutes, then gradually add the warmed milk, stirring until all the milk has been added and the mixture is quite thick.
3 Remove from heat and add seasoning, beaten egg and sufficient dried breadcrumbs to make the mixture shape easily when cold.
4 Form into rissoles and deep fry in corn oil or vegetable fat until a golden brown; drain and serve. Do not freeze.

Mushroom roast

8 oz (225g) mushrooms	1 teaspoon yeast extract
1 large onion	seasoning
2 tablespoons corn oil	1 egg
6 oz (170g) grated cheese	
4 oz (115g) dried	
wholemeal breadcrumbs	

1 Wipe the mushrooms with a damp cloth and cut into pieces.
2 Peel and chop the onion into small pieces and cook in the corn oil with the mushrooms for 15 minutes.
3 Add the grated cheese, breadcrumbs, yeast extract, seasoning and beaten egg and place in a greased baking dish.
4 Bake at 375°F/190°C (Gas Mark 5) for 30-40 minutes. Freeze when cool if desired — see paragraph at the beginning of this section.

Mushroom soufflé

8 oz (225g) mushrooms	2 eggs, separated
1 oz (30g) wholemeal flour	sea salt
2 oz (55g) butter	freshly ground black
½ pint (285ml) milk	pepper
4 oz (115g) grated cheese	

1 Wipe the mushrooms with a damp cloth, cut into small pieces and cook over a low heat in the butter for 10 minutes.
2 Add the flour and mix well in, then gradually add the warmed milk, stirring well until all the milk has been added and the mixture has thickened.
3 Remove from the heat and add the grated cheese, beaten egg yolks, sea salt and freshly ground black pepper.

4 Beat the egg whites until stiff and carefully fold into the mixture.

5 Pour into a greased soufflé dish and bake for 30-40 minutes at 350°F/180°C (Gas Mark 4) until the soufflé is well risen and golden brown. Do not freeze.

Onions au gratin

6 medium-sized onions
4 oz (115g) mushrooms
2 tablespoons corn oil
1 oz (30g) wholemeal flour

½ pint (285ml) milk
6-8 oz (170-225g) grated cheese
seasoning

1 Peel the onions and cut in half (top to bottom) and cook in water until tender, but not too soft; drain well.

2 Wipe the mushrooms with a damp cloth, cut into small pieces and cook in the corn oil for 5 minutes.

3 Add the flour and mix well in, then gradually add the warmed milk, stirring well, together with about half the grated cheese and seasoning to taste.

4 Place the onion halves in a large baking dish and pour the savoury sauce over them, sprinkling the remaining cheese over the top.

5 This savoury can be finished under the grill until the cheese topping is golden brown, or baked in a moderately hot oven, 375°F/190°C (Gas Mark 5) for about 30 minutes. Do not freeze.

Onion soufflé

2 onions
2 tablespoons corn oil
3 eggs
4 tablespoons wholemeal breadcrumbs

sea salt
freshly ground black pepper

1 Peel the onions, slice thinly and cook in the corn oil for 15 minutes.

2 Grease a baking dish and place the onion in it.

3 Separate the egg yolks and whites and mix the yolks with the breadcrumbs, salt and pepper.

4 Whisk the egg whites until very stiff and carefully fold into the mixture.

5 Pour on to the onions and bake for 30 minutes at 375°F/190°C (Gas Mark 5).

6 Serve immediately with parsley or tomato sauce. Do not freeze.

Stuffed onions

6 large onions
6 oz (170g) grated cheese
3 oz (85g) ground cashew nuts
3 oz (85g) dried wholemeal breadcrumbs

1 good teaspoon yeast extract
½ teaspoon sage
sea salt
freshly ground black pepper

1 Peel the onions and cook whole in a large pan with water until they are tender, but not too soft.

2 Remove the centres from the onions when they have cooled slightly and chop into small pieces.

3 Add the grated cheese to the chopped onion, together with the remaining ingredients and fill the centres of the onions with this mixture.

4 Place on a greased baking dish and bake in a moderately hot oven 375°F/190°C (Gas Mark 5) for 30 minutes. Do not freeze.

Vegetable paella

2 onions
3 tablespoons corn or olive oil
2 cloves garlic
8 oz (225g) brown rice
8 oz (225g) red and green peppers
4 sticks celery

1 teaspoon basil
½ teaspoon marjoram
sea salt
freshly ground black pepper
8 oz (225g) tomatoes
1 pint (570ml) vegetable stock

1 Peel the onions, cut into small pieces and cook for 10 minutes in the corn oil together with the crushed cloves of garlic.

2 Wash the rice and add, together with the de-seeded and chopped peppers, chopped celery, basil, marjoram, sea salt, freshly ground black pepper and skinned chopped tomatoes and cook for 10 minutes.

3 Add the vegetable stock and cook over a low heat until the rice and vegetables are cooked. Serve. Do not freeze.

Pea and Brazil nut cutlets

1 lb (455g) cooked peas
6 oz (170g) ground Brazil nuts
4 oz (115g) rissole powder
1 dessertspoon chopped fresh sage

sea salt
freshly ground black pepper
1 egg

1 Mash the peas well and mix in all the remaining ingredients.

2 Form into cutlets, dipping in beaten egg and breadcrumbs if desired.

3 Fry in hot corn oil or vegetable fat until golden brown; drain and serve. Cool and freeze at this stage if desired — see paragraph at the beginning of this section.

Vegetable Savouries

Pea and mint soufflé

12 oz (340g) cooked peas
½ pint (285ml) milk
1 dessertspoon chopped
   fresh mint
1 teaspoon yeast extract
sea salt
freshly ground black
   pepper
2 eggs, separated

1 Rub the peas through a sieve, or, alternatively, liquidize with the milk, mint, yeast extract, sea salt, black pepper and egg yolks.
2 Beat the egg whites until quite stiff and carefully fold into the mixture.
3 Bake in a greased soufflé dish for 30-40 minutes at 350°F/180°C (Gas Mark 4). Serve immediately. Do not freeze.

Baked pea savoury

1 onion
1 tablespoon corn oil
12 oz (340g) cooked peas
4 oz (115g) ground
   hazelnuts
2 oz (55g) dried
   wholemeal breadcrumbs
1 teaspoon yeast extract
½ teaspoon basil
sea salt
freshly ground black
   pepper
2 eggs

1 Peel and grate the onion and cook in the corn oil for 5 minutes.
2 Mash the peas and add, together with the remaining ingredients and place the mixture in a greased baking dish.
3 Bake at 375°F/190°C (Gas Mark 5) for 30 minutes. Serve with vegetables or cool and freeze if desired — see paragraph at the beginning of this section.

Potato and cheese casserole

3 onions
1½ lbs (680g) potatoes
sea salt
freshly ground black
   pepper
¼ teaspoon mace
6-8 oz (170-225g) grated
   cheese
½ pint vegetable stock
½ pint milk

1 Peel the onions and potatoes and slice them, cooking for 10 minutes in a little water; drain.
2 Grease a casserole and put layers of onion, potatoes, sea salt, pepper, mace, grated cheese, pouring the vegetable stock mixed with the milk over before adding the final topping of grated cheese.
3 Place the lid on and bake at 325°F/170°C (Gas Mark 3) for 1½ hours. Then remove the lid and cook for a further 20-30 minutes at 350°F/180°C (Gas Mark 4) until the cheese topping is golden brown. Serve hot. This savoury is best made fresh so do not freeze.

Potato and cheese rissoles

8 oz (225g) cooked
   mashed potato
8 oz (225g) grated cheese
2 oz (55g) dried
   wholemeal breadcrumbs
1 teaspoon sage
⅛ teaspoon ground
   nutmeg
sea salt
freshly ground black
   pepper
2 eggs

1 Mix all the ingredients together and form into rissoles.
2 The rissoles can be dipped in beaten egg and coated with breadcrumbs.
3 Fry in deep hot corn oil or vegetable fat until golden brown; drain and serve. Alternatively, cool and freeze — see paragraph at the beginning of this section.

Savoury potato rissoles

12 oz (340g) cooked
   mashed potato
3 oz (85g) ground
   hazelnuts
3 oz (85g) grated cheese
2 oz (55g) dried
   wholemeal breadcrumbs
½ teaspoon marjoram or
   basil
sea salt
freshly ground black
   pepper
1-2 eggs

1 Mix all the ingredients together and form into rissoles.
2 Coat with beaten egg and breadcrumbs, if desired.
3 Fry in deep hot corn oil until golden brown then drain well and serve; alternatively cool and freeze — see paragraph at the beginning of this section.

Ratatouille

3 onions
3 tablespoons corn or olive
   oil
1-2 cloves garlic
12 oz (340g) courgettes
8 oz (225g) tomatoes
2 green peppers
1 teaspoon dried parsley
¼ teaspoon paprika
   pepper
sea salt
6-8 oz (170-225g) grated
   Cheddar cheese

1 Peel the onions, cut into small pieces and cook in the corn oil or olive oil with the crushed garlic for 10 minutes.
2 Add the sliced courgettes, the skinned and chopped tomatoes and the de-seeded and chopped green peppers. Cook over a low heat for 30 minutes. Freeze at this point if desired.
3 Add the dried parsley and seasoning to taste.
4 Serve with grated cheese sprinkled over. It can be served with cooked brown rice to make a very satisfying meal.

Vegetable soufflé

1 onion	*½ teaspoon oregano*
2 tablespoons corn or olive	*sea salt*
oil	*freshly ground black*
1-2 cloves garlic	*pepper*
6 oz (170g) courgettes	*3 eggs*
1 red pepper	
6 oz (170g) aubergine	

1 Peel the onion, cut into small pieces and cook in the corn oil with the crushed garlic for 15 minutes.
2 Add the diced courgettes, de-seeded and diced red pepper and the diced aubergine and cook for 15 minutes.
3 Add the oregano and seasoning and remove from the heat.
4 Separate the egg whites and yolks and add the yolks to the mixture.
5 Whisk the egg whites until quite stiff and carefully fold into the mixture.
6 Place in a greased soufflé dish and bake at 375°F/190°C (Gas Mark 5) for 30 minutes. Serve immediately it is cooked. Do not freeze.

Shepherd's pie

2 onions	*freshly ground black*
2 tablespoons corn oil	*pepper*
¾ pint (425ml) water	*4 oz (115g) grated cheese*
6 oz (170g) tvp mince	*1½-2 lb (680-900g)*
(natural flavour)	*potatoes*
½ teaspoon sage	*2 tablespoons tomato*
½ teaspoon marjoram	*purée*
sea salt	

1 Peel the onions, cut into small pieces and cook in the corn oil for 15 minutes.
2 Add the water and tvp mince, together with the sage, marjoram, sea salt, black pepper and cook for 10 minutes.
3 Place in a greased baking dish.
4 Add the grated cheese to the seasoned mashed potatoes and divide into two halves, adding the tomato purée to one half.
5 Cover the savoury with alternative lines of pink and white mashed potato and mark with a fork. Freeze at this stage if desired, defrosting for 2-3 hours at room temperature and then proceed with the baking.
6 Bake at 375°F/190°C (Gas Mark 5) for 30 minutes, until the potato is nicely browned.

Stuffed peppers

3 large peppers — red,	*bulgar wheat, millet or*
green or yellow	*savoury stuffing*

1 Cut the peppers in half; de-seed them and cook in boiling water for 2 minutes.
2 Stuff with one of the three stuffings and place on a greased baking dish and bake for 30 minutes at 400°F/200°C (Gas Mark 6). Do not freeze.

Bulgar wheat stuffing

1 large onion	*½ teaspoon rosemary*
1 tablespoon corn oil	*herbs*
½ pint (285ml) tomato	*sea salt*
juice	*freshly ground black*
3 oz (85g) bulgar wheat	*pepper*
3 oz (85g) ground	
hazelnuts	

1 Peel the onion, cut into small pieces and cook in the corn oil for 15 minutes.
2 Add the tomato juice and bulgar wheat and cook over a low heat for 20 minutes, adding more tomato juice if required.
3 Add the remaining ingredients and use to stuff the peppers.

Millet stuffing

4 oz (115g) mushrooms	*½ teaspoon basil*
2 tablespoons corn oil	*½ teaspoon sage*
4 oz (115g) millet flakes	*sea salt*
¼ pint (140ml) water	*freshly ground black*
4 oz (115g) grated cheese	*pepper*

1 Wipe the mushrooms with a damp cloth, cut into small pieces and cook in the corn oil for 5 minutes.
2 Add the millet flakes and water and cook for 10 minutes, adding more water if necessary.
3 Add the remaining ingredients, mix well and use to stuff the peppers.

Savoury stuffing

4 sticks celery	*1 teaspoon yeast extract*
2 cloves garlic	*½ teaspoon sage*
2 tablespoons corn oil	*2 oz (55g) rissole powder*
3 oz (85g) ground	*sea salt*
hazelnuts	*freshly ground black*
	pepper

1 Wash the celery, cut into small pieces; crush the cloves of garlic and cook the celery and garlic in the corn oil for 20 minutes over a low heat.
2 Liquidize the cooked celery and garlic and then add the remaining ingredients. Mix well and use to stuff the peppers.

Vegetable Savouries

Tomato, egg and cheese soufflé

12 oz (340g) tomatoes	sea salt
1 oz (30g) butter or	freshly ground black
vegetable margarine	pepper
6 oz (170g) grated cheese	2 eggs, separated
½ teaspoon oregano	

1 Cook the tomatoes in the butter or margarine for 5 minutes.
2 Rub through a sieve, or liquidize to make a smooth purée.
3 Add the grated cheese, oregano, sea salt, black pepper and egg yolks.
4 Beat the egg whites until stiff and carefully fold in.
5 Pour into a greased soufflé dish and bake at 350°F/180°C (Gas Mark 4) for 30-40 minutes until well risen and golden brown. Serve immediately. Do not freeze.

Savoury stuffed tomatoes

12 large firm tomatoes	½ teaspoon basil
6 oz (170g) grated cheese	sea salt
2 oz (55g) millet flakes	freshly ground black
1 tablespoon grated onion	pepper

1 Skin the tomatoes, if desired, cut off the tops and remove the centre pulp; mix this with the remaining ingredients.
2 Fill the centres of the tomatoes with the mixture and place the tomato tops back on.
3 Lightly sprinkle extra millet flakes over the tomatoes and place on a greased baking dish.
4 Bake for 20-30 minutes at 375°F/190°C (Gas Mark 5). Do not freeze.

Bean and vegetable stew

12 oz (340g) haricot beans	1 teaspoon ground cumin
2 onions	½ teaspoon coriander
2 tablespoons corn oil	sea salt
1 red and 1 green pepper	freshly ground black
2 carrots	pepper
4 sticks celery	
½ teaspoon ground	
bayleaves	

1 Soak the beans overnight; drain and add fresh water or vegetable stock and cook for 30 minutes.
2 Peel the onions, cut into small pieces and cook in the corn oil in a large pan for 10 minutes.
3 De-seed and chop the peppers, and add to the cooking onion, together with the carrots and celery, cut into small pieces, and cook for 10 minutes.
4 Add the partly-cooked beans and water, together with the remaining seasoning ingredients and allow to cook over a low heat until the beans and vegetables are tender. Serve,

or cool and place in a container and freeze; it will keep 2-3 months. When using, thaw at room temperature and heat in a pan, or use a microwave oven.

Dumplings

2 oz (55g) margarine or	sea salt
Suenut	freshly ground black
8 oz (225g) wholemeal	pepper
self-raising flour	¼ pint (140ml) water

1 Rub the fat into the flour mixed with the salt and pepper.
2 Add sufficient water to make a dough.
3 Divide into the required number of dumplings and roll into balls.
4 Drop gently into the simmering soup or stew and cook over a low heat for 20 minutes.

Variations:
1 Add ½ cupful of grated cheese to the dumpling mixture before adding the water to make Cheese Dumplings.
2 Add various herbs to the dumpling mixture to make different types of Herb Dumplings.
3 Use tomato juice and a little tomato purée to the dry ingredients to make Tomato Dumplings.

Chestnut stew

1 lb (455g) chestnuts	1 teaspoon sweet basil
2 onions	sea salt
2 tablespoons corn oil	freshly ground black
½ lb (225g) tomatoes	pepper
1 green pepper	1 teaspoon yeast extract

1 To shell the chestnuts, slit the skins with a sharp knife and place in a hot oven for about 20 minutes.
2 Peel the onions, cut into small pieces and cook in a large pan in the corn oil for 10 minutes.
3 Add the skinned sliced tomatoes and de-seeded chopped green pepper and cook for 5 minutes.
4 Add the shelled chestnuts, together with sufficient water or vegetable stock to cover, also the sweet basil, sea salt and black pepper and cook over a low heat until the chestnuts are tender. Add the yeast extract and serve bordered with mashed potatoes. Alternatively, cool the stew and place in a container and freeze for up to 2 to 3 months. When required, thaw out at room temperature and heat in a pan or microwave oven.

Lentil stew

2 onions
2 tablespoons corn oil
½ lb (225g) carrots
½ lb (225g) potatoes
½ lb (225g) red lentils
1 pint (570ml) vegetable
   stock

1 teaspoon oregano
1 teaspoon yeast extract
sea salt
freshly ground black
   pepper

1 Peel the onions, cut into small pieces and cook in a large pan in the corn oil for 10 minutes.
2 Add the peeled and diced carrots and peeled and diced potatoes and red lentils together with the vegetable stock and oregano and cook over a low heat until the vegetables and lentils are soft.
3 Add yeast extract, sea salt and black pepper to taste. Freeze at this point if desired.

Vegetable casserole

1 lb (455g) onions
1 lb (455g) carrots
1 lb (455g) swede or
   turnips
1 lb (455g) potatoes
6 oz (170g) grated cheese
½ teaspoon sage

½ teaspoon basil
sea salt
freshly ground black
   pepper
1 teaspoon yeast extract
¾ pint (425ml) vegetable
   stock

1 Peel the onions, cut into small pieces, also the carrots and swede or turnips and slice the potatoes.
2 Place a layer of all the vegetables in a casserole and sprinkle with grated cheese, sage, basil, salt and pepper.
3 Add the remaining vegetables and cheese with seasoning, etc.
4 Dissolve the yeast extract in the vegetable stock and pour over.
5 Place a lid on a casserole and bake at 350°F/170°C (Gas Mark 4) for 1 hour.
6 Remove the lid and cook until the top is golden brown — about 45 minutes.
7 If making this casserole to freeze, omit the cheese and add when this dish has been defrosted at room temperature, before heating up — sprinkle all the cheese on top and heat under the grill.

6.
PIZZAS, PANCAKES AND PIES

PIZZAS

Wholemeal pizzas are now very popular dishes and there are many different tasty ones that can easily be made. The pizzas can be cooled and frozen when partly cooked and kept for 2-3 months in the freezer. When using, either defrost at room temperature for 2-3 hours and bake in a hot oven — 400°F/200°C (Gas Mark 6) for 20 minutes, or place straight in the oven and bake for 30 minutes. A microwave oven can be used, in which case cook for up to 10 minutes.

Pizza base

1 teaspoon Muscovado sugar
½ oz (15g) fresh yeast
⅓ pint (200ml) warm water

12 oz (340g) wholemeal flour
1 teaspoon sea salt
1 tablespoon corn or olive oil

1 Add the sugar and yeast to the warm water and stir until both have dissolved; leave to stand in a warm place for 10 minutes.
2 Mix the flour and salt and add the yeast and water mixture and oil and make into a soft dough.
3 Place in a bowl covered with a damp cloth in a warm place to rise for 30-40 minutes, until the dough has doubled in size.
4 Use to make 3 large pizza bases or 6 smaller pizza bases, rolling the dough out quite thinly and placing either in round greased sandwich tins or on a large baking tray. The bases are now ready for adding the pizza topping.

Quick pizza base

4 oz (115g) vegetable margarine
12 oz (340g) wholemeal flour

½ teaspoon sea salt
1 tablespoon corn or olive oil
cold water or milk to mix

1 Rub the margarine into the flour and salt.
2 Add the oil and sufficient liquid to make a soft dough.
3 Roll out and use as required, making three large or six small pizza bases.

Scone pizza base

12 oz (340g) wholemeal self-raising flour
3 oz (85g) vegetable margarine

1 tablespoon corn oil
4 tablespoons milk

1 Rub the margarine into the flour, adding a little sea salt if desired.
2 Make into a soft dough with the corn oil and milk.
3 Divide into three to make three large size pizza bases or into six to make smaller bases and roll out fairly thin.

Variation: Tomato juice can be used in place of milk in making this recipe; also for a change, 2-3 ounces (55-85g) grated cheese can be added to make a savoury cheese base.

Mixed vegetable pizza

1 large onion
2 tablespoons corn or olive
  oil
1-2 cloves garlic
4 oz (115g) aubergine
1 red pepper
4 oz (115g) carrot
4 oz (115g) courgettes

4 oz (115g) mushrooms
½ teaspoon mixed herbs
½ teaspoon oregano
sea salt
freshly ground black
  pepper
pizza bases (see page 44)

1 Peel the onion, cut into small pieces and cook in the oil with the crushed garlic cloves for 10 minutes.
2 Dice the aubergine; de-seed the pepper and cut into small pieces, peel and dice the carrot; chop the courgettes and the mushrooms and add to the onion and cook for 15 minutes.
3 Add the herbs, oregano, salt and pepper; mix well and spread over the bases.
4 Bake at 400°F/200°C (Gas Mark 6) for 20-30 minutes. Serve immediately, or cool and freeze — see paragraph at the beginning of this section.

Mushroom pizza

1 large onion
2 tablespoons corn or olive
  oil
12-16 oz (340-455g)
  mushrooms
1 teaspoon oregano
1 teaspoon basil

sea salt
freshly ground black
  pepper
8 oz (225g) grated cheese
black olives to garnish
pizza bases

1 Peel the onion, cut into small pieces and cook in the oil for 10 minutes.
2 Wipe the mushrooms and cut into small pieces and add to the cooking onion and cook for 5 minutes.
3 Add the oregano, basil and seasoning to taste and when cool spread the mixture over the pizza bases.
4 Sprinkle with grated cheese — Cheddar, Double Gloucester, or Mozzarella and place the olives on top.
5 Bake at 400°F/200°C (Gas Mark 6) for 20-30 minutes. Serve immediately.

Onion pizza

1 tablespoon corn or olive
  oil
6 oz (170g) grated cheese
3 onions
6 tomatoes

sea salt
freshly ground black
  pepper
pizza bases

1 Make 3 large pizzas or six smaller ones.
2 Brush the pizza rounds with a little oil and then sprinkle with grated cheese.
3 Peel the onions, slice quite thinly and spread evenly on the cheese-covered pizza bases.
4 Skin the tomatoes and place slices between the slices of onions, adding sea salt and black pepper to taste.
5 Brush a little oil over the top of each pizza and bake at 400°F/200°C (Gas Mark 6) for about 30 minutes.

Note: It is preferable to use vegetarian cheese, Cheddar, Double Gloucester or Red Leicester are all good to use.

Onion and mushroom pizza

2 onions
2 tablespoons corn or olive
  oil
2 cloves garlic
8 oz (225g) mushrooms
1 teaspoon basil

1 teaspoon oregano
sea salt
freshly ground black
  pepper
8 oz (225g) grated cheese
pizza bases

1 Peel the onions, cut into small pieces and cook for 10 minutes in the oil with the crushed cloves of garlic.
2 Cut the mushrooms into small pieces and add to the onions and cook for 5 minutes, adding the basil, oregano, sea salt and black pepper.
3 Spread the mixture on to the pizza bases and sprinkle the cheese on top.
4 Bake at 400°F/200°C (Gas Mark 6) for 20-30 minutes. Serve immediately, or cool, wrap and freeze. (See commencing paragraph to this section.)

Pepper pizza

1 large onion
1 tablespoon corn or olive
  oil
1 clove garlic
3 peppers, (red, green and
  yellow)
4 oz (115g) tomatoes

1 teaspoon oregano
sea salt
freshly ground black
  pepper
8 oz (225g) grated cheese
pizza bases

1 Peel the onion, cut into small pieces and cook in the oil with the crushed clove of garlic for 5 minutes.
2 De-seed the peppers and cut into small pieces and add to the onion, together with the skinned sliced tomatoes, and cook for 5 minutes.
3 Add the oregano and seasoning to taste and spread over the pizza bases.
4 Sprinkle with grated cheese and bake at 400°F/200°C (Gas Mark 6) for 20-30 minutes. Serve immediately, or cool and freeze according to instructions at beginning of this section.

Pizzas, Pancakes and Pies

Ratatouille pizza

2 medium sized onions	½ teaspoon oregano
2 tablespoons corn or olive	½ teaspoon basil
oil	sea salt
2 cloves garlic	freshly ground black
1 green or yellow pepper	pepper
4 courgettes	pizza bases
8 oz (225g) tomatoes	8 oz (225g) grated cheese

1 Peel the onions, cut into small pieces and cook for 5 minutes in the oil with the crushed cloves of garlic.
2 De-seed the pepper, cut into small pieces and add to the cooking onion together with the chopped courgettes and cook for 5 minutes.
3 Skin the tomatoes and add, together with the oregano, basil, sea salt and pepper and cook for a few minutes.
4 Spread the mixture over the pizza bases and cover with grated cheese.
5 Bake at 400°F/200°C (Gas Mark 6) for 20-30 minutes. Serve immediately, or cool and freeze wrapping the pizzas well.

BATTERS AND PANCAKES
Here are a few ideas using 100% wholemeal flour for making delicious savoury puddings and pancakes. There are of course many many more recipes using only wholefood ingredients that are very appetizing. The savoury puddings are not to be recommended for freezing — they are better made fresh and served immediately they are cooked.

It is possible to freeze pancakes with or without fillings. When made, cool, wrap them and freeze, keeping for two to three months in the freezer. Defrost at room temperature and then fry in hot corn oil until heated through. They can also be placed in the hot fat straight from the freezer, allowing longer cooking time.

Almond batter pudding

4 oz (115g) wholemeal	½ pint (285ml) milk
flour	sea salt
3 oz (85g) ground almonds	freshly ground black
2 eggs	pepper

1 Place all the ingredients in a liquidizer and blend for one minute.
2 Alternatively, make the batter using an egg whisk, placing all the ingredients into a bowl and whisking until very smooth.
3 Allow to stand for about 1 hour.
4 Place a little oil in six round baking tins and place in a hot oven for a few minutes to allow the oil to get hot.
5 Pour equal quantities of the batter into each tin and bake at 425°F/220°C (Gas Mark 7) for about 20 minutes, until the puddings are risen and golden brown. Serve immediately, with jacket potatoes, vegetables, gravy, etc.

Nut dumplings in batter

Yorkshire pudding batter	Nut dumplings
4 oz (115g) wholemeal	1 onion
flour	1 tablespoon corn oil
2 eggs	4 oz (115g) ground
½ pint (285ml) milk	hazelnuts
sea salt	2 oz (55g) wholemeal
	breadcrumbs
	½ oz (15g) wholemeal
	flour
	½ teaspoon sage
	sea salt
	freshly ground black
	pepper

1 Make the pudding batter (see recipe below) and leave to stand for 1 hour.
2 Peel the onion, grate finely and cook in the corn oil for 5 minutes.
3 Add the remaining ingredients and form into balls.
4 Place a little oil in one large baking tin and place in a hot oven for a few minutes to allow the oil to get hot.
5 Pour the batter into the tin and place the savoury balls evenly in the batter.
6 Bake at 425°F/220°C (Gas Mark 7) for 20-30 minutes. Serve immediately.

Savoury Yorkshire pudding

4 oz (115g) wholemeal	½ pint (285ml) milk
flour	sea salt
2 eggs	1 red or green pepper

1 Place the flour, eggs, milk and sea salt in a liquidizer and mix for one minute; alternatively, place all the ingredients in a large jug and whisk until smooth.
2 Allow to stand for 1 hour, then whisk again.
3 De-seed the pepper and cut into small pieces and add to the batter.
4 Place a little corn oil into one large or two or three smaller baking tins and place in a hot oven for two minutes.
5 Pour the batter into the tin or tins and bake at 425°F/220°C (Gas Mark 7) for 20-30 minutes. Serve immediately.

Variations:
1 Use six *Sausalatas* sliced into fairly thin slices in place of the pepper — adding the slices of *Sausalatas* to the batter after it has been poured into the baking tin or tins.
2 Use cubes of any kind of nutmeat in place of the pepper, adding the same way as the *Sausalatas*.
3 Use whole cashew nuts sprinkled into the batter after pouring it into the baking tin or tins.

Pancake batter

2 eggs
½ pint (285ml) milk
4 oz (115g) wholemeal
flour

sea salt
corn oil

1 Place all the ingredients except the corn oil in a liquidizer and mix for 1 minute; alternatively place all the batter ingredients in a large jug and whisk well with an egg whisk.
2 Allow to stand for up to 1 hour.
3 Heat a little corn oil in a frying pan and when hot, pour sufficient batter in to cover the bottom of the pan.
4 When golden brown underneath, turn over and cook the second side.
5 Serve plain as a pudding with a little lemon juice and raw cane sugar, or stuffed as a savoury.

Onion and courgette pancake filling

1 large onion
1 clove garlic
1 tablespoon corn oil
4 courgettes
½ teaspoon thyme or basil

sea salt
freshly ground black
pepper
1 dessertspoon wholemeal
flour

1 Peel the onion, cut into small pieces and cook in the corn oil with the crushed clove of garlic for 5 minutes.
2 Chop the courgettes into small pieces and add to the onion, together with the herbs, salt and pepper and cook for 15 minutes, or until the onion and courgettes are soft.
3 Add the flour by sprinkling it on to the cooking onion and courgettes and stirring into the mixture.
4 Use to stuff the pancakes when cooked and serve immediately, or keep warm on a warm plate in the oven. Alternatively, cool, wrap and freeze; see paragraph at the start of this section.

Mushroom pancake filling

8 oz (225g) mushrooms
2 tablespoons corn oil
1 oz (30g) wholemeal flour
¼ pint (140ml) milk

½ teaspoon mixed herbs
sea salt and freshly
ground black pepper

1 Wipe the mushrooms, cut into small pieces and cook for 5 minutes in the corn oil.
2 Add the flour and mix well in.
3 Gradually add the milk, stirring well, and finally the herbs and seasoning and use to stuff the cooked pancakes.

Variation: Add 3 oz (85g) grated cheese to make Mushroom and Cheese Filling.

FLANS AND PIES

I always recommend using all 100% wholemeal flour when making pastry. For shortcrust pastry it is best to use either cold water or cold milk to mix; using milk gives a delicious short pastry. When made, it can be wrapped and frozen and kept in the freezer until required, keeping for 2-3 months, and defrosting at room temperature. Always use plain flour when making shortcrust pastry and remember that the proportion of flour to fat is 2:1, e.g. for 8 oz (225g) flour, use 4 oz (115g) fat, for 12 oz (340g) flour, use 6 oz (170g) fat, and so on.

Wholemeal pastry

2 oz (55g) vegetable fat
2 oz (55g) vegetable
margarine

8 oz (225g) wholemeal
flour
cold water or milk to mix

1 Rub the fat and margarine well into the flour, and lightly mix in the liquid to form a dough.
2 Allow to rest in a cool place, well covered, for about 20 minutes before using.

Note: You can use 4 oz margarine, rather than half margarine and half vegetable fat.

Rolled oat pastry

4 oz (115g) vegetable
margarine
4 oz (115g) wholemeal
flour

4 oz (115g) rolled oats
1 egg

1 Rub the margarine into the flour; add the rolled oats and mix well in.
2 Form into a light dough with the beaten egg.
3 To use, press into a greased flan tin. Prick the bottom well and bake in a hot oven — 400°F/200°C (Gas Mark 6), for 10 minutes before adding the filling. When cool, the part-baked flan cases can be frozen and kept in the freezer for 2-3 months, until required. Defrost at room temperature and add filling and bake.

Millet pastry

4 oz (115g) vegetable
margarine
4 oz (115g) wholemeal
flour

4 oz (115g) millet flakes
1 egg

1 Rub the margarine well into the flour; add the millet flakes and make into a light dough with the beaten egg.
2 Press into a greased flan tin. Prick the bottom well and bake at 400°F/200°C (Gas Mark 6) for 10 minutes before adding filling, or freeze as for Rolled Oat Pastry (see recipe above).

Pizzas, Pancakes and Pies

Raised pastry

4 oz (115g) margarine
6 oz (170g) boiling water
4 oz (115g) vegetable fat

1 lb (455g) wholemeal
flour
sea salt as desired

1 Dissolve the margarine in the boiling water.
2 Rub the vegetable fat well into the flour and make into a dough with the margarine and water, adding salt as required. Allow to cool then divide into 4 to 6 pieces.
3 Using a medium-sized jam jar, block out the pastry shells for the pies.
4 Place a band of greaseproof paper round the blocked pastry shells before filling, secure with string and leave the paper on until the pastry is set (after baking about 20 minutes).
5 Alternatively, roll out the pastry carefully, using sufficient flour for the purpose, and use to line four to six baking tins.

Bean and tomato pie

shortcrust pastry made
from 12 oz (340g)
wholemeal flour (see
page 47)
8 oz (225g) haricot beans
1 onion
1 tablespoon corn oil
8 oz (225g) tomatoes

2 oz (55g) Shredded
Wheat biscuits, crushed
6 oz (170g) grated cheese
½ teaspoon sage
½ teaspoon marjoram
sea salt
freshly ground black
pepper

1 Soak the beans overnight and cook in sufficient water until tender; drain.
2 Peel the onion, cut into small pieces and cook for 10 minutes in the corn oil.
3 Skin and chop the tomatoes and add to the onion, cooking for a further 10 minutes.
4 Add the remaining ingredients, together with the cooked beans. Cool.
5 Roll out two-thirds of the pastry and line a baking dish or tin.
6 Pour the filling in and cover with the remaining pastry.
7 Bake at 400°F/200°C (Gas Mark 6) for 30-40 minutes. Serve hot, or cool and freeze, keeping for 2-3 months. Defrost at room temperature and cook in a hot oven for about 20 minutes, or up to 10 minutes in a microwave oven.

Cheese and onion flan

Millet pastry flan case (see
page 47)
2 onions
2 tablespoons corn oil
4 oz (115g) grated cheese

2 eggs
¼ pint (140ml) milk
sea salt
freshly ground black
pepper

1 Peel the onions, cut into small pieces and cook in the corn oil for 20 minutes over a low heat.
2 Add the grated cheese, beaten eggs, milk, sea salt and black pepper to taste.
3 Pour the filling into the part-baked millet pastry flan case and bake at 350°F/180°C (Gas Mark 4) for 30 to 40 minutes, until the filling is set and golden brown on top. Can be cooled and kept in the freezer for 2-3 months if desired, defrosting at room temperature and baking for the required length of time.

Cheese and mushroom flan

rolled oat pastry flan case
(see page 47)
1 onion
2 tablespoons corn oil
4 oz (115g) mushrooms
4 oz (115g) grated cheese

2 eggs
¼ pint (140ml) milk
sea salt
freshly ground black
pepper

1 Peel and finely chop the onion and cook for 10 minutes in the corn oil. Add the chopped mushrooms and cook for a further 10 minutes.
2 Add the grated cheese, beaten eggs, milk, sea salt and freshly ground black pepper. Pour the filling into the pastry flan case.
3 Bake at 350°F/180°C (Gas Mark 4) for 30 to 40 minutes until the filling is set and golden brown.

Cheese and onion pie

shortcrust pastry using 1
lb (455g) wholemeal
flour (see page 47)
4 large onions

8 oz (225g) grated cheese
sea salt
freshly ground black
pepper

1 Cook the peeled and sliced onions in a little water until nearly soft; drain well and allow to cool.
2 Line a baking dish or tin with two-thirds of the shortcrust pastry.
3 Place alternate layers of onions, grated cheese, sea salt and freshly ground black pepper in the pastry case and cover with the remaining pastry.
4 Prick the top pastry a few times with a fork (to allow the steam to escape) and bake at 400°F/200°C (Gas Mark 6) for 30-40 minutes. Serve hot, or cool and freeze, keeping in the freezer for 2-3 months. Defrost at room temperature for 2-3 hours and bake in a hot oven for 20 minutes, or up to 10 minutes in a microwave oven.

Hazelnut flan

shortcrust pastry using
  6 oz (170g) wholemeal
  flour (see page 47)
1 onion
1 tablespoon corn oil
3 oz (85g) ground
  hazelnuts
1 teaspoon yeast extract
½ teaspoon mixed herbs
2 eggs
¼ pint (140ml) milk
sea salt
freshly ground black
  pepper

1 Use pastry to line a flan tin and bake blind for 10 minutes in a hot oven 400°F/200°C (Gas Mark 6).
2 Peel the onion, cut into small pieces and cook in the corn oil for 15 minutes over a low heat.
3 Add the ground hazelnuts, yeast extract, mixed herbs, beaten eggs, milk, sea salt and black pepper.
4 Pour the filling into the flan case and bake at 375°F/190°C (Gas Mark 5) for 30-40 minutes. Serve hot, or cool and freeze, keeping for 2-3 months. Defrost at room temperature, bake in a hot oven for 20 minutes, up to 10 minutes in a microwave oven.

Lentil flan

shortcrust pastry using
  6 oz (170g) wholemeal
  flour
4 oz (115g) red lentils
1 onion
1 tablespoon corn oil
1 teaspoon yeast extract
1 egg
sea salt
freshly ground black
  pepper

1 Line a flan tin with pastry and bake blind for 10 minutes at 400°F/200°C (Gas Mark 6).
2 Wash the lentils and cook in sufficient water until soft; drain.
3 Peel the onion, cut into small pieces and cook in the corn oil for 15 minutes.
4 Add the lentils, together with the yeast extract, beaten egg, sea salt and black pepper.
5 Pour the filling into the flan case and bake for 30-40 minutes at 375°F/190°C (Gas Mark 5). Serve when cooked, or cool and freeze, keeping in the freezer for 2-3 months. Defrost at room temperature and bake for 20 minutes in a hot oven.

Mung bean flan

shortcrust pastry using
  6 oz (170g) wholemeal
  flour (see page 47)
1 onion
1 clove garlic
1 tablespoon corn oil
4 oz (115g) mung beans
2 eggs
¼ pint (140ml) milk
½ teaspoon basil
½ teaspoon sage
sea salt
freshly ground black
  pepper

1 Line a flan tin with the pastry and bake blind for 10 minutes at 400°F/200°C (Gas Mark 6).
2 Peel the onion, cut into small pieces; peel and crush the garlic and cook both in the corn oil for 15 minutes.
3 Add sufficient water to the pan to cook the mung beans for 30 minutes, until they are soft.
4 Remove from the heat and cool for a few minutes, then add the beaten eggs, milk, basil, sage, sea salt and black pepper.
4 Pour into the flan case and bake at 400°F/200°C (Gas Mark 6) for 30 minutes. Serve hot, or cool and freeze, keeping for 2-3 months. Defrost at room temperature and bake for 20 minutes in a hot oven — 400°F/200°C (Gas Mark 6).

Mushroom and cheese flan

rolled oat pastry (see
  page 47)
4 oz (115g) mushrooms
1 oz (30g) butter
4 oz (115g) grated cheese
2 eggs
½ pint (140ml) milk
⅛ teaspoon nutmeg
sea salt
freshly ground black
  pepper

1 Use the rolled oat pastry to line a flan tin and pre-bake according to the instructions on page 47.
2 Wipe the mushrooms with a damp cloth, cut into small pieces and cook in the butter for 5 minutes. Remove from heat.
3 Add the grated cheese, beaten eggs, milk, nutmeg, sea salt and black pepper.
4 Pour the filling into the part-baked flan case and bake at 375°F/190°C (Gas Mark 5) for 30 minutes, until the filling is set and golden brown. Serve hot, or cool and freeze as for Mung Bean Flan.

Pizzas, Pancakes and Pies

Onion flan

Pastry:
4 oz (115g) vegetable
  margarine
4 oz (115g) wholemeal
  flour
3 oz (85g) rolled oats
2 oz (55g) ground Brazil
  nuts
1 egg

Filling:
3 onions
2 oz (55g) vegetable
  margarine
1 teaspoon yeast extract
2 eggs
¼ pint (140ml) milk
sea salt
freshly ground black
  pepper

1 Make the pastry by rubbing the margarine into the flour, rolled oats and ground nuts; add the egg and lightly mix into a soft dough.
2 Press the pastry into a greased flan tin and bake blind for 10 minutes in a hot oven — 375°F/190°C (Gas Mark 5)
3 Peel the onions, cut into small pieces and cook in the margarine for 20 minutes over a low heat.
4 Add the yeast extract, beaten eggs, milk and seasoning and pour into the part-baked flan base.
5 Bake at 375°F/190°C (Gas Mark 5) for 30-40 minutes. Serve hot. For freezing, see Mung Bean Flan.

Onion and celery pie

Pie crust:
3 oz (85g) vegetable
  margarine
2 oz (55g) ground
  hazelnuts
1 large egg, separated
6 oz (170g) wholemeal
  flour
sea salt
freshly ground black
  pepper

Filling:
3 onions
6 celery sticks
2 tablespoons corn oil
4 oz (115g) grated cheese
sea salt
freshly ground black
  pepper

1 To make the pastry, cream the margarine and ground hazelnuts, then add the egg, flour and seasoning.
2 Line a greased baking dish using two-thirds of the pastry.
3 Peel the onions, cut into small pieces and cut the celery into small pieces and cook in the corn oil for 20 minutes; alternatively, cook the onions and celery in water and drain when cooked.
4 Place a layer of grated cheese on the pastry, then the cooked onions and celery and cover with the remaining cheese and season.
5 Cover with the remaining pastry and bake at 400°F/200°C (Gas Mark 6) for 30-40 minutes. Serve hot with gravy, jacket potatoes, etc., or cool and freeze and keep for up to 3 months, defrosting at room temperature for 2-3 hours. Bake for 20 minutes at 400°F/200°C (Gas Mark 6).

Raised vegetable pies

1 quantity raised pastry
  (see page 47)
1 large onion
6 oz (170g) swede
6 oz (170g) carrots
4-6 celery sticks
6 oz (170g) peas

1 oz (30g) bulgar wheat
1 teaspoon yeast extract
⅛ teaspoon coriander
sea salt
freshly ground black
  pepper

1 Peel the onion, cut into small pieces; peel the root vegetables and cut into small pieces; wash the celery and also cut into small pieces.
2 Place the onion, root vegetables, celery and peas in a pan with sufficient water to cook for 20 minutes.
3 Add the bulgar wheat and cook for 20 minutes, or until it is cooked.
4 Add the yeast extract, coriander, sea salt and black pepper; allow to cool.
5 Place the filling into the raised pastry shells and cover with pastry rounds, securing the edges well.
6 Bake at 400°F/200°C (Gas Mark 6) for 30 minutes. Serve when baked, or cool and freeze; they will keep 2-3 months in the freezer well wrapped. Defrost at room temperature for 2-3 hours and bake for about 20 minutes at 400°F/200°C (Gas Mark 6) or up to 10 minutes in a microwave oven.

Rice and cheese flan

wholemeal pastry flan
  case (see page 47)
2 oz (55g) brown rice
1 onion
1 oz (30g) vegetable
  margarine
4 oz (115g) grated cheese

1 teaspoon curry powder
½ teaspoon turmeric
sea salt
freshly ground black
  pepper
1 egg

1 Use pastry to line a flan tin and bake blind at 400°F/200°C (Gas Mark 6) for 10 minutes.
2 Wash the rice and cook in sufficient water until tender.
3 Peel the onion, grate and cook for 5 minutes in the margarine.
4 Add the cooked rice to the onion, together with the remaining ingredients.
5 Place the filling into the part-baked flan case and bake at 375°F/190°C (Gas Mark 5) for 30-40 minutes. Serve, or cool and freeze if desired, as for Mung Bean Flan.

Savoury rice rolls

2 oz (55g) brown rice
1 onion
1 tablespoon corn oil
2 oz (55g) grated cheese
1 teaspoon yeast extract
½ teaspoon sage
1 oz (30g) dried
    wholemeal breadcrumbs
sea salt

freshly ground black
    pepper
shortcrust pastry using
    8 oz (225g) wholemeal
    flour (see page 47)

1 Wash the rice and cook in sufficient water until soft; drain.
2 Peel the onion, cut into small pieces and cook for 20 minutes in the corn oil over a low heat.
3 Add the rice to the cooked onion, together with the remaining ingredients; allow to cool. (Rissole powder can be used in place of dried breadcrumbs.)
4 Roll the pastry out in long strips, fairly thin and place the filling along the length; moisten the edges with water and fold the pastry over, securing the edges well.
5 Brush with a little milk or beaten egg if desired and cut into small rolls.
6 Bake at 400°F/200°C (Gas Mark 6) for 20-30 minutes. Serve hot; or cool and freeze, wrapping well up in freezer bags. Defrost at room temperature and bake at 400°F/200°C (Gas Mark 6) for 20 minutes; or use a microwave oven.

Savoury soya flan

4 oz (115g) soya chunks (or
    mince)
½ pint (285ml) orange or
    tomato juice
1 onion
1 tablespoon corn oil

2 eggs
sea salt
freshly ground black
    pepper
shortcrust flan case, part-
    baked (see page 47)

1 Soak the soya chunks or mince in the orange or tomato juice.
2 Peel the onion, cut into small pieces and cook in the corn oil for 10 minutes; add the soaking soya chunks or mince and cook for 20 minutes then allow to cool for a few minutes.
3 Add the beaten eggs, salt and pepper to taste and pour into the flan case.
4 Bake at 375°F/190°C (Gas Mark 5) for 30 minutes. Serve, or cool and freeze — see Mung Bean Flan.

Tomato and hazelnut flan

1 onion
2 tablespoons corn oil
1 small green pepper
⅓ pint (200ml) tomato
    juice
2 eggs
3 oz (85g) ground
    hazelnuts

½ teaspoon thyme
½ teaspoon marjoram
sea salt
freshly ground black
    pepper
shortcrust flan case, part-
    baked (see page 47)

1 Peel the onion, cut into small pieces and cook in the corn oil for 10 minutes. De-seed the pepper, cut into small pieces and add to the onion, cooking for a further 20 minutes.
2 Add the tomato juice, beaten eggs, ground hazelnuts, thyme, marjoram and seasoning to taste.
3 Pour the mixture into the part-baked pastry flan case and bake at 400°F/200°C (Gas Mark 6) for 30 minutes. Serve, or cool and freeze — see details under Mung Bean Flan (page 49).

Vegetable tarts

Pastry:
6 oz (170g) wholemeal
    flour
2 oz (55g) ground
    hazelnuts
3 oz (85g) vegetable
    margarine
water to mix

Filling:
1 onion
8 oz (225g) carrots
8 oz (225g) peas
¾ pint (425ml) vegetable
    stock
1 teaspoon yeast extract
sea salt
freshly ground black
    pepper
2 teaspoons agar-agar

1 Make the pastry by rubbing the margarine into the flour, then adding the hazelnuts and sufficient water to form a dough and roll out; line moderately deep baking tins and bake blind at 400°F/200°C (Gas Mark 6) for 15-20 minutes; cool.
2 Peel the onion, cut into small pieces; peel and dice the carrots. Cook the onion, diced carrots and peas in the vegetable stock until tender; drain.
3 Make the liquid up to ¾ pint (425ml), adding the yeast extract, seasoning and agar-agar and bring to the boil; simmer until the agar-agar has dissolved.
4 Fill the pastry cases with the vegetables and pour the liquid over until covered and leave until set.
5 Serve cold with salad. Do not freeze.

Pizzas, Pancakes and Pies

Mixed vegetable pie

2 medium sized onions
2 oz (55g) vegetable
  margarine
4 sticks celery
6 oz (170g) carrots
6 oz (170g) swede
6 oz (170g) peas
1 lb (455g) potatoes
8 oz (225g) Nuttolene

sea salt
freshly ground black
  pepper
yeast extract gravy
shortcrust pastry made
  from 12 oz (340g)
  wholemeal flour (see
  page 47)

1 Peel the onion, cut into small pieces and place in a large casserole with the margarine, chopped celery, diced carrots, diced swede and peas.
2 Place the lid on and cook in a hot oven at 400°F/200°C (Gas Mark 6) for 45 minutes, then add the peeled, chopped potatoes and cook for a further 20 minutes.
3 Add the diced *Nuttolene*, seasoning and sufficient gravy to cover.
4 Roll out the pastry and place on top. Any left over can be used to decorate the pie.
5 Bake at 400°F/200°C (Gas Mark 6) for 30-40 minutes, until the pastry is golden brown. Serve with green vegetables, green beans, gravy, etc. Do not freeze.

Millet, cheese and onion pie

Pastry:
8 oz (225g) wholemeal
  flour
4 oz (115g) millet flakes
6 oz (170g) vegetable
  margarine
2 oz (55g) grated cheese
water to mix

Filling:
3-4 onions
8 oz (225g) grated cheese
1 teaspoon mixed herbs
sea salt
freshly ground black
  pepper

1 Make the pastry by rubbing the margarine into the flour, millet flakes and cheese; add sufficient water to make into a light dough.
2 Peel the onions, cut into small pieces and cook in a little water until nearly tender; drain and cool.
3 Using over half the pastry, line a baking dish and fill with layers of onion, cheese, mixed herbs and seasoning, ending with a layer of cheese.
4 Cover with the remaining pastry and bake for 30-40 minutes at 400°F/200°C (Gas Mark 6). Serve hot. This pie is best made fresh.

Millet and Brazil nut pudding

Pastry:
6 oz (170g) vegetable
  margarine
8 oz (225g) wholemeal
  flour
4 oz (115g) millet flakes
water to mix

Filling:
4 onions
3 tablespoons corn oil
4 oz (115g) ground Brazil
  nuts
1 dessertspoon yeast
  extract
1 teaspoon sage
sea salt
freshly ground black
  pepper

1 Make the pastry by rubbing the margarine into the flour and millet flakes; then add sufficient water to make a light dough.
2 Peel the onions, cut into small pieces and cook in the corn oil over a low heat for 30 minutes; alternatively, the onions can be cooked in a little water and then drained.
3 Mix together the onions and all the remaining ingredients. Line a deep pudding dish with two-thirds of the pastry and place the filling in.
4 Cover with the remaining pastry. Place a piece of greaseproof paper on top then cover with baking foil or cloth, etc. Steam for 2 hours. Remove the cloth or foil and greaseproof paper and bake in a hot oven 400°F/200°C (Gas Mark 6) for 20-30 minutes. Serve.
4 This savoury can be baked in a baking dish instead of steaming, in which case bake for 30-40 minutes at 400°F/200°C (Gas Mark 6). Do not freeze.

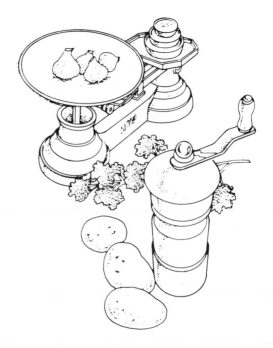

7

SALAD, MOULDS AND SPREADS

SALADS

One good salad a day is very important in providing a really healthy diet. With the very great variety of vegetables, fruits, nuts, etc. there are ample ingredients to make many different appetizing salads. It is important to make a large proportion, if not all the salad, from fresh uncooked vegetables and fruits, using cooked vegetables occasionally to add variety. Always make the salad just before the meal is ready to serve, and do not use too much dressing, so that you can really taste the ingredients. Also, it is worth spending a little time making the salads as decorative as possible, cutting radishes and tomatoes, in fancy shapes, etc.

Mixed bean salad

4 oz (115g) mung beans
4 oz (115g) haricot beans
4 oz (115g) red kidney
  beans
3 tablespoons corn or olive
  oil
1 tablespoon lemon juice
sea salt
freshly ground black
  pepper

2 tablespoons chopped
  chives
2 tablespoons chopped
  parsley
lettuce leaves
slices of tomato and
  cucumber

1 Soak the beans overnight; drain and cook in sufficient fresh water until soft; drain.
2 Mix the oil, lemon juice, sea salt and black pepper, adding ½ teaspoon mustard if desired. Also add the chopped chives and parsley and mix the dressing with the beans. Allow to cool.
3 Place on lettuce leaves in a serving bowl and decorate with slices of tomato and cucumber.

Beetroot and lettuce salad

6 oz cooked beetroot
1 large lettuce

6 large tomatoes, sliced
½ large cucumber, sliced

1 Grate or slice the beetroot.
2 Place the washed, well-drained lettuce leaves in a large flat dish, and add the beetroot, arranging in the centre of the lettuce leaves.
3 Decorate with slices of tomato and cucumber round the edge.

Note: Beetroot has a less 'earthy' taste when cooked, but it can be grated raw — if desired — with grated raw apple mixed with it: this makes a very good salad.

Butter bean salad

8 oz (225g) butter beans
1 dessertspoon grated
  onion
mayonnaise

parsley
lettuce
watercress
slices of tomato

1 Soak the beans overnight; drain and add sufficient fresh water to cook until tender; drain well.
2 Add the grated onion to the mayonnaise together with the chopped parsley and mix well with the beans; allow to cool.
3 Place the beans on a serving dish covered with lettuce leaves and surround the beans with chopped watercress and slices of tomato.

Salad, Moulds and Spreads

Celery and date salad

6-8 celery sticks
mayonnaise or salad
  dressing
lettuce leaves

18-24 fresh dates
8 oz (225g) cottage cheese
6 tomatoes

1 Wash the celery and chop fairly small; mix with the mayonnaise or salad dressing and place on a dish of lettuce leaves. (A little chopped apple and/or chopped nuts can be added to the celery for variation.)
2 Wash the dates, remove the stones and stuff with cottage cheese; place round the salad, together with slices of tomato. (As an alternative to cottage cheese, the dates can be stuffed with ground hazelnuts, Brazil nuts, etc., mixed with a little mayonnaise.)

Chicory and tomato salad

1 lb (455g) chicory
1 teaspoon grated
  horseradish

mayonnaise
lettuce leaves
8 oz (225g) tomatoes

1 Wash the chicory and chop fairly finely.
2 Add the grated horseradish to the mayonnaise and mix with the chopped chicory.
3 Arrange the lettuce leaves on a flat dish and pile the chicory in the centre with slices of tomato round the dish.

Cream cheese and carrot salad

1 lettuce
1-2 bunches watercress
chopped chives
12-16 oz (340-455g) cream
  cheese

12 oz (340g) grated carrots
a little olive oil and lemon
  juice
6 tomatoes

1 Place the lettuce leaves and watercress on a large salad plate.
2 Add the chopped chives to the cream cheese and place in the centre of the lettuce leaves and watercress.
3 Arrange the grated carrots round the cream cheese and pour a little oil and lemon juice over the carrots.
4 Decorate with slices of tomato and/or sliced cucumber if desired.

Egg and cucumber salad

6-9 hard-boiled eggs
1 medium-sized cucumber
lettuce leaves

chives
mayonnaise
6 tomatoes

1 Slice the hard-boiled eggs and cucumber and arrange on a plate covered with lettuce leaves.
2 Add the finely chopped chives to the mayonnaise and cover the slices of egg and cucumber with it.
3 Decorate with slices of tomato.

Health salad

½ medium-sized cabbage
2 large carrots
2 raw beetroots
1 large cooking apple

8 oz (225g) ground Brazil
  nuts
6 tomatoes
French dressing

1 Shred the cabbage; grate the carrots and then grate the beetroots and cooking apple together.
2 Arrange in three sections round a dish — covered with lettuce leaves if desired — and place the ground Brazil nuts in the centre.
3 Decorate with quarters of tomato and serve with French dressing.

Potato and tomato salad

1½-2 lb (680-900g) new
  potatoes
chopped chives
chopped parsley

mayonnaise
lettuce leaves
a little mustard and cress
6 large tomatoes

1 Cook the new potatoes until tender (about 15 minutes), and remove the skins when they have cooled slightly; cut into slices.
2 Add the chopped chives and chopped parsley to the mayonnaise, and pour over the slices of potato, mixing well together.
3 Place the potatoes on a plate of lettuce leaves and decorate with mustard and cress and slices of tomato.

Rice salad

12-16 oz (340-455g) brown
   rice
1 large onion
4 oz (115g) red and green
   peppers
4 oz (115g) diced cucumber
6 tablespoons salad
   dressing

1 dessertspoon cider
   vinegar
sea salt
freshly ground black
   pepper
1 tablespoon chopped
   parsley

1 Wash the rice and cook over a low heat with just sufficient water until tender; drain well.
2 Peel the onion and chop very finely; de-seed the pepper and cut into small pieces. Add the onion, peppers and diced cucumber to the rice.
3 Add the remaining ingredients except the parsley and mix well in; allow to cool.
4 Place the rice in a bowl and garnish with fresh chopped parsley.

Variations:
1 In place of chopped peppers and diced cucumber, use cooked peas, diced carrots and chopped tomato.
2 Alternatively, chopped cashew nuts, diced cucumber and chopped tomato can be used.

Spanish salad

lettuce leaves
chicory leaves
2 Spanish onions
12 oz (340g) grated cheese

2 large oranges
12 olives
mayonnaise
chopped mint leaves

1 Arrange the lettuce leaves and chicory on a large serving plate.
2 Peel the onion, slice quite finely and place on the lettuce and chicory, and place the grated cheese in the centre.
3 Decorate with slices of orange and olives.
4 Serve with mayonnaise to which has been added some finely chopped fresh mint.

Tomato and beetroot salad

6 large tomatoes
4 cooked beetroots
lettuce leaves
mustard and cress

lemon, oil and honey
   dressing (see page 56)

1 Slice the tomatoes, with or without the skins, and slice the beetroot.
2 Cover a plate with lettuce leaves and arrange the slices of tomato and beetroot on it.
3 Decorate with a little mustard and cress and pour the dressing over; alternatively, the dressing can be served separately.

Mixed vegetable salad

12 oz (340g) cooked
   chopped celery
12 oz (340g) cooked diced
   carrots
12 oz (340g) cooked diced
   potatoes
12 oz (340g) cooked peas

chopped parsley
a little grated onion
mayonnaise
mustard and cress
slices of tomato and
   cucumber

1 Mix all the vegetables together.
2 Add the chopped parsley and grated onion to the mayonnaise and mix in with the vegetables.
3 Serve on a bed of mustard and cress and decorate with slices of tomato and cucumber.

Vitamin salad

1 lb (455g) carrots
1 lb (455g) cabbage
1 large onion
2 tablespoons corn or olive
   oil
1 tablespoon lemon juice

lettuce leaves
slices of tomato and
   cucumber
mustard and cress

1 Shred the carrots, cabbage and onion and mix together with the oil and lemon juice, (cider vinegar can be used in place of the lemon juice).
2 Arrange the lettuce leaves on a plate and add the shredded vegetables.
3 Decorate with slices of tomato, cucumber and mustard and cress.

Winter salad

1 lettuce
6-8 celery sticks
yogurt dressing (see page
   56)

2 large carrots
2 medium-sized beetroots
6 tomatoes

1 Wash the lettuce and drain well. Arrange the leaves over a large plate.
2 Wash the celery and cut into small pieces and mix with the yogurt dressing. Place in the centre of the lettuce leaves.
3 Grate the carrots and the uncooked beetroots separately and place in alternative heaps round the celery, and garnish with slices of tomato.

Salad, Moulds and Spreads

French dressing

8 tablespoons olive or corn oil
4 tablespoons lemon juice
sea salt
freshly ground black pepper

1 Mix all the ingredients well together and use as required.

Note: A little mustard and/or a pinch of raw cane sugar can be used in this dressing if liked. Also, cider vinegar can be used to replace the lemon juice.

Lemon, oil and honey dressing

8 tablespoons olive oil
4 tablespoons lemon juice
2 tablespoons clear honey

1 Mix all the ingredients well together, either using an electric liquidizer, or place in a bowl and whisk very well. Alternatively, place in a jar with a screw-top lid and shake very well.

Mayonnaise

2 egg yolks
1 teaspoon mustard
1 teaspoon raw cane sugar
sea salt
½ pint (285ml) olive oil
lemon juice or cider vinegar

1 Mix the egg yolks, mustard, raw cane sugar and sea salt together.
2 Very gradually add the oil, mixing well.
3 When the mixture becomes thick, add a little lemon juice or cider vinegar.
4 Continue adding the oil gradually and the lemon juice or cider vinegar, until all the oil has been used.
5 Add sufficient lemon juice or cider vinegar to make the mayonnaise the required consistency.

Salad dressing

1 teaspoon each of wholemeal flour, raw cane sugar and mustard
½ teaspoon sea salt
2 egg yolks
1 tablespoon olive oil
2 tablespoons lemon juice
1 cup milk

1 Add the flour, sugar, mustard, salt and egg yolks to the olive oil and mix well.
2 Slowly add the lemon juice and then lastly the milk.
3 Pour the mixture into a double boiler and cook until the dressing thickens, stirring well.
4 If this dressing is mixed as directed, it will not curdle. Pour whilst still warm into a jar and cool until needed.

Yogurt dressing

5 fl oz (140ml) natural yogurt
1 dessertspoon lemon juice
½ teaspoon mustard

1 Mix all the ingredients well together and use as required. A liquidizer can be used to mix this dressing.

SAVOURY MOULDS

Various savoury moulds can be made using either agar-agar or *Gelozone* to set them. The following are just a few ideas for delicious savoury moulds using wholesome ingredients.

Savoury nutmeat mould

1 large tin Nuttolene
2 good teaspoons agar-agar
2 pints (1.13 litres) vegetable stock
1 good teaspoon yeast extract
sea salt
freshly ground black pepper

1 Dice the nutmeat quite small and place in a mould that has been rinsed out with cold water.
2 Dissolve the agar-agar in the vegetable stock and add the yeast extract and seasoning to taste; allow the liquid to boil for 2 minutes.
3 Pour the liquid over the diced nutmeat and leave overnight, or until cold and completely set. Serve sliced with salad.

Hazelnut mould

1 heaped teaspoon agar-agar
1 pint (570ml) vegetable stock
1 good teaspoon yeast extract
½ teaspoon sage
sea salt
freshly ground black pepper
2 oz (55g) ground hazelnuts
2 oz (55g) rissole powder

1 Dissolve the agar-agar in the vegetable stock, bringing to the boil and boiling gently for 2-3 minutes.
2 Add the yeast extract, sage, sea salt, black pepper, ground hazelnuts and rissole powder.
3 To obtain a very smooth mixture, use a liquidizer before pouring into a mould rinsed out with cold water.
4 Leave overnight, or until fully set. Turn out and serve with salad.

Savoury cheese mould

1 onion
1 tablespoon corn oil
14 oz (395g) tin tomato
  juice
3 teaspoons Gelozone
4 oz (115g) grated cheese

⅛ teaspoon nutmeg
sea salt
freshly ground black
  pepper
1 egg, separated

1 Peel the onion, grate finely and cook in the corn oil for 10
  minutes.
2 Add the tomato juice, reserving a little to mix with the
  Gelozone, and heat until it is boiling.
3 Dissolve the *Gelozone* in the reserved tomato juice and add
  to the boiling tomato juice, stirring until it dissolves.
4 Add the grated cheese, stirring until it has melted, then add
  the nutmeg, sea salt, black pepper and allow to cool for a
  few minutes.
5 Add the beaten egg yolk and mix well in — using a liquidizer
  if desired.
6 Beat the egg white until stiff and fold into the mixture.
7 Pour into a mould rinsed out with cold water.
8 If desired, the dish can be decorated with thin slices of tomato
  or cucumber before the mixture is poured in. Leave to set.
9 To serve, turn out on to a plate covered with lettuce leaves.

Tomato and cheese mould

8 oz (225g) tomatoes,
  chopped
1 oz (30g) vegetable
  margarine
¼ pint (140ml) vegetable
  stock
1 heaped teaspoon
  agar-agar

6 oz (170g) grated cheese
½ teaspoon sage
⅛ teaspoon mace
sea salt
freshly ground black
  pepper

1 Cook the tomatoes in the margarine for 5 minutes, then rub
  through a sieve, or use a liquidizer.
2 Return to the pan with the vegetable stock and agar-agar and
  bring to the boil. Allow to boil for a minute or two until the
  agar-agar has dissolved.
3 Add the grated cheese, sage, mace and seasoning and mix
  well until the cheese has melted.
4 Pour into a mould that has been rinsed out with cold water
  and leave until set.
5 Serve on a bed of lettuce leaves and surround with slices of
  cucumber.

Brazil nut mould

1 medium-sized onion
1 tablespoon corn oil
1 pint (570ml) vegetable
  stock
1 heaped teaspoon
  agar-agar

1 good teaspoon yeast
  extract
sea salt
freshly ground black
  pepper
4 oz (115g) ground Brazil
  nuts

1 Peel the onion, grate finely and cook in the corn oil for 10
  minutes.
2 Add the vegetable stock and powdered agar-agar, together
  with the yeast extract, sea salt and black pepper. Bring to
  the boil to dissolve the agar-agar.
3 Add the ground Brazil nuts and cook over a low heat for a
  few minutes before pouring into a mould that has been rinsed
  out with cold water.
4 Leave until set. Turn out and serve sliced with salad.

SANDWICH PASTES
There are many very tasty vegetarian sandwich pastes that can
be made. Use them with home-made wholemeal bread or rolls,
with or without various salads, to make very satisfying
sandwiches. The following pastes will keep longer if kept in
the refrigerator.

Almond sandwich paste

1 medium-sized onion
2 tablespoons corn oil
4 oz (115g) soya flour

4 oz (115g) ground
  almonds
1 dessertspoon Marmite

1 Liquidize the peeled and chopped onion and corn oil and
  place them in a pan.
2 Cook for 5 minutes, then add the soya flour, ground almonds
  and *Marmite* and allow to cook for a further 5 minutes.
3 Place in a jar when cool.

Bean paste

4 oz (115g) butter beans
1 onion
2 oz (55g) butter or
  vegetable margarine
4 oz (115g) ground nuts

1 teaspoon yeast extract
sea salt
freshly ground black
  pepper

1 Soak the beans overnight; drain and add fresh water and cook
  until soft; drain and mash the beans.
2 Peel the onion, grate finely and cook in the butter or vegetable
  margarine for 5 minutes.
3 Add the mashed beans, together with the remaining
  ingredients and cook for a few minutes.
4 Cool and place in a jar.

Salad, Moulds and Spreads

Cheese paste

4 oz (115g) butter
4 tablespoons milk

4 oz (115g) grated cheese
1 dessertspoon Marmite

1 Melt the butter in a saucepan with the milk.
2 Add the grated cheese and stir until it has melted, then add the *Marmite*.
3 Cool slightly and then place in a jar. (It will be a few hours before this paste is ready for use.)

Cheese and tomato sandwich paste

3 large tomatoes
2 oz (55g) butter or
vegetable margarine
1 tablespoon grated onion
2 oz (55g) rissole powder

2 oz (55g) grated cheese
1 egg
sea salt
freshly ground black
pepper

1 Skin the tomatoes, cut into pieces and cook in the butter or margarine with the grated onion for 5 minutes.
2 Add the remaining ingredients and cook over a low heat, stirring, until the mixture thickens. Cool and place in a jar.

Lentil sandwich paste

1 large onion
2 oz (55g) vegetable
margarine
4 oz (115g) red lentils
4 oz (115g) grated cheese

1 dessertspoon yeast
extract
sea salt
freshly ground black
pepper

1 Peel the onion, grate finely and cook in the margarine for 5 minutes.
2 Add the washed lentils and a little water and cook for about 30 minutes, stirring occasionally.
3 When cooked, add the remaining ingredients.
4 If the mixture is a little too soft, add a few dried wholemeal breadcrumbs or rissole powder whilst still cooking the paste. Cool and place in a jar.

Lentil and nut paste

1 onion
2 oz (55g) butter
4 oz (115g) red lentils
4 oz (115g) ground nuts
1 good teaspoon yeast
extract

sea salt
freshly ground black
pepper

1 Peel the onion, grate finely and cook in the butter for 5 minutes.

2 Add the lentils and just sufficient water; cook until the lentils are soft and fairly dry.
3 Add the ground nuts, yeast extract and seasoning to taste.
4 Cool and place in a jar.

Pine kernel paste

2 onions
2 oz (55g) butter or
vegetable margarine
4 oz (115g) ground pine
kernels
1 good teaspoon yeast
extract

½ teaspoon sage
sea salt
freshly ground black
pepper
a few dried wholemeal
breadcrumbs

1 Peel the onions, grate finely and cook in the butter or margarine for 10 minutes.
2 Add the remaining ingredients and cook over a low heat for a few minutes, adding a few dried wholemeal breadcrumbs to make a spreading paste.
3 Cool and place in a jar; use immediately it is cool.

Note: Other nuts can be used in place of the pine kernel nuts.

Quick tomato cheese paste

2 oz (55g) butter or
vegetable margarine
8 oz (225g) grated cheese
3 tablespoons tomato
purée

sea salt
freshly ground black
pepper

1 Cream the butter or margarine and mix thoroughly with the remaining ingredients.

Note: Tomato ketchup can be used in place of tomato purée.

Tomato and cheese spread

8 oz (225g) tomatoes
1 oz (30g) vegetable
margarine
4 oz (115g) grated cheese
1 teaspoon Gelozone

1 tablespoon tomato purée
sea salt
freshly ground black
pepper

1 Skin and chop the tomatoes and cook in the margarine for 5 minutes.
2 Add the grated cheese.
3 Dissolve the *Gelozone* in a little cold water and add to the paste mixture, together with the tomato purée, sea salt and black pepper.
4 Stir until the mixture comes to the boil; remove from the heat and allow to cool. Place in a jar and use as required, storing in a cool place.

8.

HOT PUDDINGS AND COLD DESSERTS

HOT PUDDINGS

When planning satisfying wholesome menus, a hot pudding makes a pleasant change from fresh fruit or a cold pudding, especially on a chilly day. Undoubtedly fresh fruit is always excellent for serving after the main course but, especially with a growing family, hot or cold puddings or desserts are always very popular. Try to use plenty of fruit in making some of the puddings. Following are a few ideas using wholesome ingredients. Most puddings are best made fresh.

Apple and almond custard

½ pint (285ml) milk
4 oz (115g) raw cane sugar
l lb (455g) dessert apples
2 oz (55g) ground almonds
1 oz (30g) Shredded
  Wheat *crumbs*
2 eggs

1 Heat the milk and dissolve the sugar in it.
2 Peel and chop the apples.
3 Grease a baking dish and place a layer of apple, then a layer of ground almonds mixed with the *Shredded Wheat* crumbs; continue with layers of apple, nut and crumb mixture, finishing with a layer of nuts and crumbs.
4 Beat the eggs and milk together and pour over the apple layers.
5 Bake for about 45 minutes at 350°F/180°C (Gas Mark 4) when the pudding is ready to serve.
6 Serve with a little cream or *Plamil Delice*, etc. Do not freeze.

Baked apples

6 large cooking apples
2 oz (55g) ground hazelnuts
4 oz (115g) raisins
1 tablespoon honey

1 Wash the apples, remove the core and fill the centres with ground hazelnuts, raisins and honey.
2 Place on a greased baking dish and bake at 375°F/190°C (Gas Mark 5) for 30 minutes, or until the apples are soft.
3 Serve with cream or *Plamil Delice*, etc. Baked apples can be frozen, when cool, if desired. Place in a container, separating the apples, storing for 2-3 months in the freezer. Defrost at room temperature for 2-3 hours and bake for 20 minutes.

Apple soufflé pudding

1 lb (445g) cooking apples
½ oz (15g) vegetable margarine
3 oz (85g) Demerara sugar
2 eggs, separated
¼ teaspoon cinnamon

1 Peel the apples, core and slice.
2 Melt the margarine in a pan and add the sliced apples and sugar and cook slowly over a low heat.
3 When cooked to a pulp, remove from the heat and cool slightly before adding the two beaten egg yolks and cinnamon.
4 Beat the egg whites till very stiff, fold into the mixture and place in a greased soufflé dish.
5 Bake at 350°F/180°C (Gas Mark 4) for 30-40 minutes, when the pudding should have risen well and set.
6 Serve immediately with cream *Plamil Delice* or thin custard. Do not freeze.

Hot Puddings and Cold Desserts

Apple and mincemeat charlotte

stale wholemeal bread
butter or vegetable
  margarine
6 oz (170g) mincemeat

1 lb (445g) apples
2 oz (55g) Muscovado
  sugar

1 Grease a baking dish and line with slices of buttered wholemeal bread.
2 Cover with a thin layer of mincemeat, then a layer of peeled sliced apples and sugar.
3 Put another layer of mincemeat on top of the apples and then the remaining apples and sugar.
4 Place thin slices of buttered bread on top and bake at 375°F/190°C (Gas Mark 5) for 30 minutes.
5 Serve with custard or cream. Do not freeze.

Apple and hazelnut sponge

1 lb (455g) apples
2 oz (55g) Muscovado
  sugar

Sponge:
4 oz (115g) vegetable
  margarine
4 oz (115g) Muscovado
  sugar
2 eggs
2 oz (55g) wholemeal flour
2 oz (55g) ground
  hazelnuts

1 Peel, core and chop the apples and cook in a pan over a low heat with the Muscovado sugar until nearly soft.
2 Place the apples in a greased baking dish. (If desired, the apples can be cut into small pieces and placed uncooked into the baking dish with the sugar.)
3 To make the sponge: beat the margarine and Muscovado until light; then gradually add the beaten eggs, mixing well.
4 Finally fold in the flour and ground hazelnuts and place the sponge mixture over the apples.
5 Bake at 400°F/200°C (Gas Mark 6) for 30 minutes.
6 Serve with custard, cream or *Plamil Delice*. This pudding is best made fresh, although it could be frozen if desired and kept 2-3 months, defrosting at room temperature for 2-3 hours and then baking in a hot oven for 20 minutes.

Baked fruit sweet

1½ lb (680g) cooking
  apples
4 oz (115g) Demerara
  sugar

2 oz (55g) vegetable
  margarine
4 oz (115g) wholemeal
  breadcrumbs

1 Peel the apples, chop into small pieces and cook in a pan with half the sugar until soft.
2 Place the cooked apples in a greased baking dish.
3 Rub the margarine into the breadcrumbs and add the remaining sugar and place this mixture on top of the apples.
4 Bake at 375°F/190°C (Gas Mark 5) for 30 minutes.
5 Serve with custard, evaporated milk, plantmilk etc. Do not freeze.

Note: This sweet can be varied by cooking the apples with some seedless raisins or other dried fruit; alternatively, use other types of fruit.

Christmas pudding

8 oz (225g) Suenut
8 oz (225g) wholemeal
  flour
8 oz (225g) wholemeal
  breadcrumbs
½ teaspoon mixed spice
¼ teaspoon cinnamon
2 oz (55g) ground almonds
8 oz (225g) Barbados
  sugar

8 oz (225g) raisins
8 oz (225g) currants
8 oz (225g) sultanas
4 oz (115g) candied peel
1 medium-sized apple,
  grated
1 lemon
4 eggs
milk

1 Rub the *Suenut* into the flour, breadcrumbs, spices and ground almonds.
2 Add the sugar, the washed and dried raisins, currants and sultanas; also the candied peel, grated apple and a little grated lemon rind and the juice.
3 Add the beaten eggs and sufficient milk until the mixture is a soft dropping consistency.
4 Use two greased pudding basins, filling three-quarters full; cover with greaseproof paper and cooking foil.
5 Steam for 10 hours, or boil for 8 hours. Cool and store in a cool place.
6 Steam for 3 hours when ready to use, serving with hot custard or cream.

Note: Quantities in this recipe are sufficient to serve 12-18 people.

Christmas pudding-light

6 oz (170g) Suenut
8 oz (225g) wholemeal
   breadcrumbs
8 oz (225g) Demerara
   sugar
6 oz (170g) raisins
6 oz (170g) sultanas
4 oz (115g) mixed peel
4 eggs
1 teaspoon mixed spice
1 orange
1 lemon
a little milk

1 Rub the *Suenut* into the breadcrumbs; add the sugar, washed raisins and sultanas, mixed peel, beaten eggs and mixed spice and mix well.
2 Add a grated orange and lemon rind and the juice.
3 Add a little milk if necessary and place the mixture into one large or two smaller greased pudding basins and cover with a circle of greaseproof paper; then cover with kitchen foil and/or a pudding cloth and steam for 6 hours. Cool and store in a cool place until required.
4 When using, steam for 2 hours before serving with vanilla sauce, custard, *Plamil Delice*, etc.

Coconut egg custard

1½ pints (850ml) milk
3 oz (85g) Demerara sugar
3 oz (85g) desiccated
   coconut
3 eggs

1 Heat the milk and dissolve the sugar in it.
2 Add the coconut and beaten eggs and place in a greased baking dish.
3 Bake at 350°F/180°C (Gas Mark 4) until the custard is set.
4 Serve with fresh or cooked fruit. Do not freeze.

Fruit and almond charlotte

1½ lb (680g) cooking
   apples
3 oz (85g) raisins
6 oz (170g) wholemeal
   breadcrumbs
3 oz (85g) ground almonds
1 lemon
3 oz (85g) Demerara sugar

1 Peel, core and cut the apples into small pieces.
2 Wash the raisins (and chop them if large ones are used).
3 Butter a baking dish and place a layer of breadcrumbs mixed with the ground almonds in, then a layer of apples, raisins, a little grated lemon rind and juice and sugar.
4 Repeat the layers until all the ingredients have been used, finishing with a layer of breadcrumbs and almonds.
5 Cover the top with small pieces of butter and bake at 350°F/180°C (Gas Mark 4) for 45 minutes.
6 Serve with *Plamil Delice*, cream, etc. Do not freeze.

Fruit crumble

1½ lb (680g) cooking
   apples
4 oz (115g) raisins
4 oz (115g) Demerara
   sugar
¼ teaspoon cinnamon
6 oz (170g) wholemeal
   flour
3 oz (85g) vegetable
   margarine

1 Peel the apples, cut into small pieces and place in a greased baking dish with the raisins, half the Demerara sugar and the cinnamon.
2 To make the topping, rub the margarine into the flour and add the remaining sugar; sprinkle over the fruit.
3 Bake at 350°F/180°C (Gas Mark 4) until the topping is nicely browned.
4 Serve with custard, *Plamil Delice*, etc. If this pudding is made in a suitable dish, it can be frozen if desired and kept well wrapped in the freezer for 2-3 months. Defrost at room temperature for about 3 hours and then bake for 20 minutes.

Honey sponge pudding

4 oz (115g) vegetable
   margarine
4 oz (115g) Muscovado
   sugar
2 eggs
6 oz (170g) wholemeal
   self-raising flour
2 tablespoons honey

1 Cream the margarine and sugar until light.
2 Gradually add the beaten eggs, mixing well in; fold in the flour.
3 Place the honey at the bottom of a well-greased pudding basin and add the pudding mixture on top of the honey.
4 Cover with greased greaseproof paper and foil and steam for 1½ hours.
5 Turn out and serve with custard or cream. Do not freeze.

Lemon pudding

4 oz (115g) vegetable
   margarine
4 oz (115g) Muscovado
   sugar
2 eggs
6 oz (170g) wholemeal
   self-raising flour
1 lemon

1 Cream the margarine and sugar till light.
2 Add the beaten eggs gradually, mixing well in.
3 Fold in the flour, grated lemon rind and juice.
4 Place the mixture in a greased pudding basin and cover with greased greaseproof paper and cooking foil.
5 Steam for 2 hours; turn out and serve with custard or cream. Do not freeze.

Hot Puddings and Cold Desserts

Variations:
1 In place of the lemon, add 1 good teaspoon ground ginger to make Ginger Pudding.
2 Place a tablespoonful of raw sugar jam in the bottom of the greased pudding basin before adding the mixture, with or without the lemon to make Jam Sponge Pudding.

Nutty fruit crumble

1-1½ lbs fruit (apples, pears, plums, apricots)	*4 oz (115g) wholemeal flour*
6 oz (170g) Muscovado sugar	*2 oz (55g) rolled oats*
4 oz (115g) vegetable margarine	*2 oz (55g) desiccated coconut*

1 Prepare the chosen fruit by peeling if necessary and cutting into small pieces; place in a greased baking dish with half the sugar.
2 Prepare the crumble by rubbing the margarine into the flour, rolled oats and coconut; add the sugar and mix well together.
3 Place the crumble mixture on top of the fruit.
4 Bake at 350°F/180°C (Gas Mark 4) for 30-40 minutes, when the fruit should be cooked and the topping nicely browned. Serve with cream or custard. Alternatively, if baked in a suitable dish, cool and freeze, keeping for 2-3 months. Defrost at room temperature for 2-3 hours and bake in the oven for 20 minutes.

Orange soufflé pudding

3 oz (85g) vegetable margarine	*1 large orange*
6 oz (170g) Muscovado sugar	*3 oz (140g) wholemeal self-raising flour*
3 eggs	*¾ pint (425ml) milk*

1 Cream the margarine and sugar until quite light.
2 Separate the egg white and yolks and add the yolks to the creamed margarine and sugar, together with the grated orange rind and flour.
3 Add the orange juice gradually, then add the milk, stirring well to make the mixture smooth.
4 Beat the egg whites quite stiff and carefully fold into the mixture.
5 Bake in a greased soufflé dish at 350°F/180°C (Gas Mark 4) for about 40 minutes. Serve immediately.

Variation: Replace the orange rind and juice with lemon rind and juice to make Lemon Soufflé Pudding.

Baked sponge puddings

2 eggs	*Natural vanilla essence*
3 oz (85g) Muscovado sugar	*1 oz (30g) melted vegetable margarine*
3 oz (85g) wholemeal flour	

1 Separate the egg whites and yolks and whisk the whites until very stiff, then whisk in the yolks and Muscovado sugar and continue whisking until the whisk leaves ridges in the mixture.
2 Carefully fold in the flour and add the vanilla flavouring; lastly add the melted margarine.
3 Three parts fill well-greased bun tins and bake at 400°F/200°C (Gas Mark 6) for 15-20 minutes.
4 Serve with custard, *Plamil Delice*, fresh fruit, cream etc. Do not freeze.

Apple layer pudding

Suenut pastry:	*Filling:*
12 oz (340g) wholemeal flour	*12 oz (340g) cooking apples*
6 oz (170g) Suenut	*2 oz (55g) raisins*
cold water to mix	*4 oz (115g) Demerara sugar*
	2 oz (55g) ground almonds
	1 lemon

1 Make the pastry by rubbing the *Suenut* well into the flour; add sufficient cold water to make a dough. Leave the dough covered in a cool place for a while before rolling out.
2 Line a pudding basin with two-thirds of the pastry.
3 Peel, core and chop the apples.
4 Place layers of apples, raisins, sugar, ground almonds, lemon rind and juice into the pastry-lined basin.
5 Cover with the remaining pastry, pressing the edges well together.
6 Cover with greased greaseproof paper and kitchen foil or pudding cloth and steam for 2 hours.
7 Remove foil and greaseproof paper and place in a hot oven 400°F/200°C (Gas Mark 6) for 10 minutes, then serve with custard or cream. This pudding is best made fresh.

Cherry pudding

Suenut pastry:	*Filling:*
12 oz (340g) wholemeal flour	*1 lb (455g) Morello cherries*
6 oz (170g) Suenut	*4 oz (115g) Muscovado sugar*
cold water to mix	

1 Make as for Apple Layer Pudding (see preceding recipe), substituting the cherries and sugar for the filling.

COLD DESSERTS

Fresh fruit is the best dessert from the nutritional point of view, but it does not always have to be the main choice. There are many wholesome desserts that can quite easily be made.

It is always best to make the cold desserts fresh, or just one day before serving and keep in the refrigerator until ready to serve. Experiment by substituting different fruits or ground nuts in the recipes given to make alternative desserts. Quantities given are sufficient for 6 people.

Almond snow

2 good teaspoons Gelozone	1 pint (570ml) milk a few drops natural
2 oz (55g) ground almonds	almond essence
2 oz (55g) Muscovado sugar	2 eggs, separated

1 Mix the *Gelozone*, ground almonds and sugar with a little cold milk until smooth.
2 Heat the remaining milk until near boiling and pour on to the *Gelozone* ground almonds and sugar mixture.
3 Return to the pan and, whilst stirring, cook for a few minutes; allow to cool for 15 minutes and then add the almond essence and beaten egg yolks.
4 Beat the egg whites until stiff and carefully fold them into the mixture.
5 Pour into a wetted mould and leave until set.
6 Turn out and serve with fresh fruit salad or other fruit.

Apple meringue

2 large cooking apples	2 lemons
4 oz (115g) Muscovado sugar	3-4 egg whites

1 Peel the apples, grate, and mix with the sugar, the juice of the lemons and a little grated rind.
2 Beat the egg whites until quite stiff and fold into the mixture.
3 Place in a greased baking dish and bake for 20-30 minutes at 350°F/180°C (Gas Mark 4).
4 Serve immediately with cream, or custard made with the egg yolks.

Apricot lemon jelly

1 lb (455g) fresh apricots	2 teaspoons agar-agar
4 oz (115g) Muscovado sugar	1 lemon

1 Cook the apricots in just sufficient water with the sugar until soft.
2 Drain the liquid from the apricots and add the agar-agar to this liquid; bring to the boil and when the agar-agar has all dissolved, remove from the heat.
3 Add the juice of the lemon and a little grated rind.
4 Slice about half the apricots and place in a mould that has been rinsed out with cold water, pour the liquid over and leave until set.
5 Turn the jelly out on to a plate and decorate with the remaining apricots. Serve with cream or ice-cream.

Chocolate mousse

6 oz (170g) plain chocolate	3 eggs, separated
2 tablespoons pineapple juice	pineapple pieces

1 Melt the chocolate in a bowl over a pan of hot water.
2 Remove from the heat and add the pineapple juice and egg yolks.
3 Beat the egg whites until quite stiff and carefully fold into the mixture.
4 Place in individual glasses and chill in the refrigerator.
5 Decorate with pineapple pieces and, if desired, a little whipped cream.

Custard jelly

2 level teaspoons agar-agar	2 egg yolks
¼ pint (140ml) boiling water	2 oz (55g) Muscovado sugar
¾ pint (425ml) milk	natural vanilla essence

1 Dissolve the agar-agar in the boiling water.
2 Heat the milk in a double saucepan until nearly boiling.
3 Pour the hot milk gradually over the beaten eggs and sugar and return to the pan; stir until the mixture thickens and add the dissolved agar-agar and vanilla essence.
4 Allow to cool slightly, stirring, before pouring into a wetted mould.
5 Place in the refrigerator when cool. Turn out when required and serve with fresh fruit.

Hot Puddings and Cold Desserts

Fresh fruit salad

1 large grapefruit
3 dessert apples
3 pears
3 bananas

juice of two large oranges
2 oz (55g) Muscovado sugar

1 Peel the grapefruit, remove all the pith and cut into small pieces.
2 Peel the apples and pears if desired, and cut into small pieces.
3 Peel and slice the bananas.
4 Dissolve the sugar in a little boiling water and add the orange juice; pour the liquid over the fruit.
5 Serve with a little fresh cream, nut cream or *Plamil Delice.*

Fruit salad jelly

2 bananas
2 dessert apples
2 pears
1 pint (570ml) pineapple juice

2 level teaspoon agar-agar
2 oz (55g) Muscovado sugar

1 Rinse out two moulds with cold water (or one very large one) and place layers of sliced bananas, apples and pears in them.
2 Heat the pineapple juice in a pan with the agar-agar and sugar and bring to the boil; allow to cook for 2-3 minutes until the agar-agar has dissolved. Pour over the fruit.
3 Leave until cold, keeping in the refrigerator and turn out when serving. Serve with cream, ice-cream, cold custard, etc.

Fruit trifle

1 large tin unsweetened pineapple
2-3 apples
2-3 pears
2-3 bananas

2 oranges
1 large grapefruit
⅓ pint (200ml) whipping cream

1 Drain the juice from the tinned pineapple and cut the fruit into small pieces.
2 Peel the apples and pears and cut into small pieces; peel and slice the bananas.
3 Peel the oranges and grapefruit; remove the pith and cut into pieces.
4 Place all the fruit in a large bowl and pour the fruit juice (drained from the tin of pineapple) over — this may be sweetened with Muscovado sugar or honey; add more pineapple juice to make sufficient to cover the fruit.
5 Whip the cream and decorate the top of the trifle with same.
6 Decorate with halves of green and black grapes with the seeds removed.

Note: This recipe will serve 10-12 people.

Ground rice snow and fruit

1 pint (570ml) milk
2 oz (55g) ground brown rice
2 oz (55g) Muscovado sugar

pure vanilla essence
2 egg whites
fresh fruit

1 Take a little cold milk and mix the ground rice to a smooth paste.
2 Place the remainder of the milk in a pan to heat, and when it is near boiling pour in the ground rice and cold milk and stir well; cook over a low heat for about 15 minutes, stirring until the mixture thickens.
3 Add the sugar and vanilla essence and remove from the heat.
4 Allow to cool for 15-20 minutes before carefully folding in the stiffly beaten egg whites.
5 Divide between individual glasses and leave till cool.
6 Decorate as required with fresh fruit.

Hazelnut summer pudding

Sponge cake:
3 eggs
6 oz (170g) Muscovado sugar
3 oz (85g) wholemeal flour
3 oz (85g) ground hazelnuts

Filling:
12-16 oz (340-455g) sweetened cooked raspberries or strawberries

1 Make the hazelnut sponge cake a day or two before required for use if possible, according to the instructions for Hazelnut Sponge Cake on page 77.
2 Line a greased pudding basin (bottom and sides) with the hazelnut sponge cake, leaving sufficient cake to cover the top.
3 Place the warm cooked fruit into the lined basin and cover with the remaining sponge cake. Place a plate on top with a heavy weight on it and leave overnight.
4 Turn out and decorate with whipped cream and a few fresh raspberries or strawberries.

Lemon and grape jelly

2 lemons
¾ pint (425ml) water
2 good teaspoons
  agar-agar

3 oz (85g) Muscovado
  sugar
small bunch of grapes

1 Add the lemon juice and a little grated rind to the water, together with the agar-agar and bring to the boil.
2 Boil for a minute or two, until all the agar-agar has dissolved, then add the sugar.
3 Rinse a mould out with cold water and pour the liquid into same.
4 Leave until the jelly is just beginning to set, then add the grapes, using seedless ones if available, or removing the seeds from the grapes.
5 Serve when the jelly is quite set, decorated if desired with whipped cream.

Note: Individual jellies can be made and these will set much quicker.

Lemon or orange foam

3 eggs
4 oz (115g) Muscovado
  sugar

2 large lemons or oranges

1 Separate the egg yolks from the whites and beat the yolks well.
2 Add the sugar, juice and a little of the grated rind of the lemons or oranges.
3 Place over a pan of boiling water and stir until the mixture becomes thick and creamy. Remove the basin from the pan of boiling water.
4 Fold in the stiffly beaten egg whites and place in individual glasses.
5 Serve when cold.

Muesli

4-6 oz (115-170g) rolled
  oats
pineapple juice
3 oz (85g) ground nuts

4 apples
2 oz (55g) raisins
honey

1 Soak the rolled oats in pineapple juice (or alternatively water or milk) for half an hour.
2 Add the ground nuts, grated apples, raisins and a little honey if desired and mix well. Serve.

Variation: In place of grated apple, substitute 4-6 mashed bananas mixed with a little lemon juice.

Orange moulds

2 teaspoons powdered
  agar-agar
¾ pint (425ml) hot water
2 oz (55g) Muscovado
  sugar

2 medium-sized oranges
1 lemon
1 egg white
2 bananas

1 Dissolve the agar-agar in the hot water by bringing to the boil.
2 Add the sugar and a little grated orange rind.
3 Remove from the heat and add the juice of the 2 oranges and the lemon and leave to cool for a few minutes.
4 Beat the egg white until very stiff and add to the cooling liquid folding in carefully.
5 Rinse small moulds with cold water and slice the bananas into them.
6 Pour the liquid over the bananas and leave to set.
7 When set, turn out and decorate with a little whipped cream and/or slices of fresh orange.

Prune and apple fluff

6 oz (170g) dried prunes
2 dessert apples

2 egg whites

1 Soak the prunes overnight and then cook together with the chopped apples, using only very little water.
2 Remove the prune stones and rub the prunes and apples through a sieve, or liquidize.
3 Beat the egg whites until quite stiff and fold into the prune and apple mixture.
4 Serve in individual dishes and decorate with a few flaked almonds.

Raspberry mousse

1 lb (455g) raspberries
a little less than ¼ pint
  (120ml) water
3 oz (85g) Muscovado
  sugar

3 level teaspoons
  agar-agar
2 eggs, separated

1 Cook the raspberries with the water and rub through a sieve; or use a liquidizer first, then put through a sieve.
2 Return to the pan and add the sugar and agar-agar and bring to the boil to dissolve the agar-agar; remove from the heat.
3 Allow to cool for about 15 minutes and then add the beaten egg yolks.
4 Beat the egg whites until quite stiff and carefully fold into the raspberry mixture; pour into a mould that has been rinsed out with cold water.
5 Turn out when completely set and serve with a little fresh cream or plantmilk, as desired.

Hot Puddings and Cold Desserts

Fresh fruit sponge flan

Sponge:
3 eggs
3 oz (85g) Muscovado
    sugar
3 oz (85g) wholemeal flour

Fruit filling:
slices various fresh fruit or
    raspberries, strawberries
¼ pint (140ml) fruit juice
2-3 oz (55-85g) Muscovado
    sugar
1 heaped teaspoon
    powdered arrowroot

1 Make the sponge flan by whisking the eggs and sugar until very light, then carefully fold in the flour.
2 Pour the sponge mixture into a large greased and floured flan tin.
3 Bake at 400°F/200°C (Gas Mark 6) for 15-20 minutes. Then cool on a wire tray.
4 Carefully arrange the selected fruit in the sponge flan.
5 Heat the fruit juice, sugar and arrowroot and stir until it thickens.
6 Pour over the fruit in the flan and leave until set. Serve decorated with whipped cream.

Variation:

Pineapple sponge flan

1 Drain the juice from a tin of unsweetened pineapple pieces and place the pieces in the flan case.
2 Heat the pineapple juice and add 1 heaped teaspoonful powdered arrowroot and 1 tablespoon honey. Bring to the boil and when clear, pour over pineapple pieces.

Raspberry mousse flan

1 tin unsweetened
    raspberries
2 oz (55g) Muscovado
    sugar

1 teaspoon agar-agar
1 egg white
1 baked sponge flan (see
    recipe for Sponge at top
    of page)

1 Sieve the raspberries and place in a pan with the sugar and agar-agar.
2 Slowly bring the raspberry purée to the boil and allow to boil for 1-2 minutes to dissolve the agar-agar.
3 Remove from the heat and cool for 20-30 minutes.
4 Beat the egg white until very stiff and fold into the raspberry purée.
5 Place the mousse mixture in the freezer for 1 hour before filling the sponge flan just before serving.
6 Decorate with a few whole raspberries or sliced bananas and a little piped whipped cream.

Sponge cake trifle

wholemeal sponge cake
raspberry jam
½ pint (285ml) fruit juice
3 bananas

Custard:
1 pint (570ml) milk
2 eggs
⅓ cup Muscovado sugar
natural vanilla essence
cream or grated coconut
    cream

1 Make the sponge cake according to the recipe in Summer Fruit Pudding (see page 67), but bake in a cake tin a day or two before required.
2 Cut the sponge cake and spread with reduced-sugar raspberry jam; cut the cake into pieces and place in a large bowl.
3 Heat about ½ pint fruit juice and pour same over the sponge cake.
4 Peel and cut about 3 bananas into slices and place on top of the soaked sponge cake.
5 Make the custard by whisking the milk, eggs, sugar and vanilla essence together in a bowl over a pan of boiling water and stirring until it thickens. Remove from the heat immediately and pour through a sieve over the sponge cake and sliced bananas.
6 Decorate with whipped cream or grated coconut cream.

Strawberry and almond shortcake

4 oz (115g) butter
6 oz (170g) wholemeal
flour
2 oz (55g) ground almonds
3 oz (85g) Muscovado
sugar

1 egg yolk
a little milk
1 lb (455g) strawberries
whipped cream

1 Rub the butter well into the flour. Add the ground almonds and sugar and make into a dough with the egg yolk and a little milk.
2 Divide the dough into two equal portions and roll out to fit a medium-sized sandwich tin.
3 Grease the two sandwich tins and line with greaseproof paper. Place the rounds of dough in the tins, pricking well all over.
4 Bake at 350°F/180°C (Gas Mark 4) for 20-30 minutes, until the shortcake is golden brown.
5 When cool, sandwich together with the strawberries — sweetened if desired, leaving a few strawberries to decorate the top together with some whipped cream.

Summer fruit pudding

Sponge cake:
3 eggs
6 oz (170g) Muscovado
sugar
6 oz (170g) wholemeal
flour
pure vanilla essence

Fruit filling:
1 lb (455g) any fresh fruit
3-4 oz (85-115g)
Muscovado sugar

1 Make the sponge cake about 2 days before required for making the pudding. Separate the egg yolks and whites and beat the whites until quite stiff. Add the egg yolks and sugar and beat until mixture is light, then fold in the flour and vanilla essence. Bake, in a well-greased deep round cake tin or two sandwich tins, for 40 minutes at 325°F/170°C (Gas Mark 3).
2 Line a greased pudding basin with slices of sponge cake, until the bottom and sides are well covered.
3 Cook the fruit with sufficient sugar, using very little water.
4 Pour the cooked fruit into the lined basin and cover with more sponge cake.
5 Place a plate on top, slightly smaller than the top of the basin and place a weight on top; leave overnight.
6 Turn out and serve with cream or plantmilk.

9

PIES AND BREADS

PIES

When making large or small pies for dessert, I use mainly shortcrust pastry made with 100% wholemeal flour, and occasionally puff pastry made with 100% wholemeal flour, although sometimes I do use 85% or 81% wholemeal flour, or a mixture of flours. Pastry can be well wrapped and frozen when made and kept in the freezer for future use. Defrost at room temperature for 2-3 hours, when the pastry can be rolled out. Alternatively, the cooked pies can be cooled and frozen, wrapping them to keep in the freezer for 2-3 months. To use, defrost at room temperature for 2-3 hours and then bake in a hot oven 400°F/200°C (Gas Mark 6) for 20 minutes. Serve hot or cold.

Sweet shortcrust pastry

8 oz (225g) wholemeal flour	1 oz (30g) Muscovado sugar
4 oz (115g) vegetable margarine	water or milk to mix

1 Rub the margarine well into the flour.
2 Dissolve the sugar in the water or milk and add to make into a dough.
3 Allow to stand for a few minutes in a cool place covered with cling film, then use as required.

Wholemeal puff pastry

8 oz (225g) firm vegetable margarine	½ cup cold water
8 oz (225g) wholemeal flour	1 teaspoon lemon juice

1 Rub 1 oz (30g) of the margarine into the flour.
2 Make into a dough with the water and lemon juice and allow to stand for 15 minutes, covered with a damp cloth.
3 Roll the dough out into an oblong shape.
4 Place small pieces of the remaining margarine on to two-thirds of the rolled out dough, and fold the remaining third over half the dough with margarine on and fold over again.
5 Roll the dough and fold into three; repeat this process and then cover with the damp cloth and place in a cool place for 1 hour.
6 Repeat the rolling out process twice more, allowing the pastry to rest for 1 hour each time.
7 Leave covered in the refrigerator until required; alternatively store in the freezer.

Apple tart

Pastry:
4 oz (115g) vegetable
   margarine
8 oz (225g) wholemeal
   flour
2 oz (85g) Muscovado
   sugar
½ orange

Filling:
1½ lb (680g) apples
2 tablespoons honey
2 oz (55g) desiccated
   coconut
¼ teaspoon cinnamon

1 Make the pastry by rubbing the margarine into the flour; add the sugar, a little grated orange rind and sufficient juice to make into a dough.
2 Peel and core the apples and cut into small pieces; cook with the honey until soft.
3 Mix the desiccated coconut and cinnamon with the apple.
4 Roll out two-thirds of the pastry and line a large shallow tart tin.
5 Place the apple mixture on the pastry.
6 Using the remaining pastry, roll out strips to lay across the pie and bake at 375°F/190°C (Gas Mark 5) for 30-40 minutes.
7 Serve hot or cold; or when cool, wrap and freeze — see commencing paragraph.

Apple and coconut pie

shortcrust pastry made
   from 8 oz (225g)
   wholemeal flour (see
   page 68)
Filling:
1½ lb (680g) apples
2 oz (55g) Demerara sugar

Topping:
2 oz (55g) vegetable
   margarine
2 oz (55g) Demerara sugar
1 egg
2 oz (55g) rolled oats
2 oz (55g) desiccated
   coconut

1 Roll out the pastry and use it to line a moderately deep round dish.
2 Peel the apples and cook with the sugar until tender; allow to cool.
3 Place the cooked apple in the pastry-lined dish.
4 Cream the margarine and sugar and gradually add the beaten egg.
5 Add the rolled oats and desiccated coconut and place the mixture on top of the cooked apple.
6 Bake at 400°F/200°C (Gas Mark 6) for 30-40 minutes.
5 Serve hot with custard or cream; or alternatively, cool and freeze — see commencing paragraph.

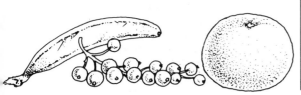

Apple flan

Flan pastry:
2 oz (55g) vegetable
   margarine
2 oz (55g) wholemeal flour
2 oz (55g) rolled oats
2 oz (55g) desiccated
   coconut
1 oz (30g) light brown raw
   cane sugar
1 egg

Filling:
½ pint (285ml) cooked
   apple
2 level teaspoons
   agar-agar
2 oz (55g) Demerara sugar
1 egg, separated
a little desiccated coconut

1 Make the pastry by rubbing the margarine into the flour, rolled oats and coconut; dissolve the sugar in the beaten egg and make the mixture into a light dough.
2 Do not roll the pastry out but press into a greased pie dish or tin. Bake blind at 400°F/200°C (Gas Mark 6) for 20-30 minutes, until golden brown.
3 Heat the apple and add the agar-agar and sugar; allow to reach boiling point to dissolve the agar-agar, cooking for 1-2 minutes.
4 Remove from heat and cool slightly before adding the egg yolk and folding in the stiffly beaten egg white.
5 Place in the cooled flan case and sprinkle with a little desiccated coconut.
6 Cut into slices when cool and set. Do not freeze.

Apple macaroon tartlets

shortcrust pastry made
   from 6 oz (170g)
   wholemeal flour (see
   page 68)
a little cooked apple
2 egg whites

3 oz (85g) fine raw cane
   sugar
2 oz (55g) ground almonds
1 tablespoon ground
   brown rice

1 Line tartlet tins with the pastry and place a small spoonful of apple into each.
2 Beat the egg whites until quite stiff.
3 Carefully stir in the sugar, ground almonds and ground rice, adding a little pure almond flavouring if desired.
4 Place a spoonful of the mixture on to each pastry-lined cavity with apple in.
5 Bake at 425°F/220°C (Gas Mark 7) for 10-15 minutes. Serve hot or cold. Do not freeze.

Pies and Breads

Coconut tartlets

shortcrust pastry made
   from 6 oz (170g)
   wholemeal flour (see
   page 68)
reduced-sugar raspberry
   jam
1 oz (30g) butter

2 oz (55g) light raw cane
   sugar
2 oz (55g) desiccated
   coconut
1 egg
natural vanilla essence

1 Line tart tins with the pastry and place a small spoonful of jam into each one.
2 Melt the butter in a saucepan and add the sugar, coconut, well beaten egg and vanilla essence.
3 Cook the mixture over a low heat for 5 minutes, stirring.
4 Place a spoonful of this mixture into each tart.
5 Bake at 400°F/200°C (Gas Mark 6) for 10-15 minutes. Serve hot or cold, or alternatively freeze when cool — see commencing paragraph.

Lemon cake layer pie

shortcrust pastry made
   from 8 oz (225g)
   wholemeal flour (see
   page 68)
2 oz (55g) butter

4 oz (115g) raw cane sugar
2 eggs
1 large lemon
2 oz (55g) wholemeal flour
¼ pint (140ml) milk

1 Line a moderately deep pie dish with the pastry.
2 Cream the butter and sugar.
3 Separate the egg yolks and whites and add the yolks to the butter and sugar, together with the grated rind and juice of the lemon.
4 Add the flour and the milk and mix well in.
5 Beat the egg whites until quite stiff and fold them into the mixture.
6 Pour into the pastry-lined pie dish and bake at 400°F/200°C (Gas Mark 6) 10 minutes, then lower the heat to 350°F/180°C (Gas Mark 4) and bake for approximately 30 minutes until the pie is firm and golden brown. The bottom part of the pie will be like a custard and the top like a wholemeal sponge cake.
7 Serve hot preferably. Do not freeze.

Mincemeat

1 lb (455g) raisins
1 lb (455g) sultanas
1 lb (455g) currants
½ lb (225g) candied peel
1 lb (455g) cooking apples
½ lb (225g) Suenut
1 lb (455g) Demerara
   sugar

2 oranges
2 lemons
1 teaspoon ground
   cinnamon
½ teaspoon ground mace
½ teaspoon mixed spice

1 Put the raisins, sultanas, currants, candied peel, peeled and cored apples, and *Suenut* through a mincer, alternately, until all have been minced.
2 Add the sugar, a little grated orange and lemon rind and the juice of the oranges and lemons, together with the spices and mix well together.
3 Place into jars, taking care not to fill the jars too full, because the mincemeat will expand slightly on keeping. Store and use as required.

Mince pies

shortcrust pastry made
   from 8 oz (225g)
   wholemeal flour (see
   page 68)

home-made mincemeat

1 Roll out the pastry and use to line tart tins.
2 Place a good spoonful of mincemeat into each tart.
3 Cover with another round of pastry and cut the top once or twice with a pair of scissors.
4 Bake in a hot oven 425°F/220°C (Gas Mark 7) for 15-20 minutes.
5 Serve hot or cold; alternatively cool, pack in freezing bags and keep in the freezer for 2-3 months.

Note: Mince pies can also be made using puff pastry.

Mincemeat squares

6 oz (170g) vegetable
   margarine
12 oz (340g) wholemeal
   flour

2 oz (55g) light raw cane
   sugar
1 egg
mincemeat

1 Rub the margarine well into the flour.
2 Dissolve the sugar in the beaten egg and add to the flour and fat; make into a dough.
3 Roll out two-thirds of the pastry and use to line a Swiss roll tin.
4 Spread a layer of mincemeat over the pastry.
5 Roll the remaining pastry out and place on top of the mincemeat, securing the edges well.
6 Prick the top well with a fork and brush with a little milk.
7 Sprinkle a little sugar on top and bake at 425°F/220°C (Gas Mark 7) for 30 minutes.
8 Serve hot or cold, or alternatively keep in the freezer until required; keeping for 2-3 months.

Banana slices

1 lb (455g) dried bananas
juice of 1 orange
juice of 2 lemons

shortcrust pastry made
from 1 lb (455g)
wholemeal flour (see
page 68)

1 Mince the dried bananas and add the fruit juice to make the bananas a soft consistency for spreading on the pastry.
2 Line a Swiss roll tin with two-thirds of the pastry and spread the filling over.
3 Cover with the remaining pastry, pressing the edges firmly together.
4 Prick the top with a fork and bake at 425°F/220°C (Gas Mark 7) for 30-40 minutes.
5 When cool, cut into slices. Freeze if required.

BREAD

Making bread at home is very easy and rewarding. There is no bread so delicious as that which is home-made, especially when 100% stone-ground flour is used. Many people think that making bread successfully is difficult, but that is not so, and I very strongly recommend home-made bread.

All bread freezes well and can be kept 3 months or even longer, if well wrapped. When the bread or rolls or teacakes are quite cool, they are ready for freezing; pack them well. When required, defrost in the wrapping at room temperature, remove the wrapping and place in a hot oven for few minutes.

Granary bread

¾ oz (20g) sea salt
2 lb (900g) granary flour
1 oz (30g) fresh yeast

16 fl oz (450ml) warm
water

1 Mix the salt into the flour.
2 Dissolve the yeast in the warm water (105°F/40°C) and make into a dough with the flour.
3 Knead the dough well for 5-10 minutes, then place in a bowl and cover with a damp cloth. Allow to rise for up to 1 hour in a warm place.
4 Knead the well-risen dough and break off into the desired size cobs, loaves or small rolls.
5 Place on warm greased baking sheets, or in greased tins, and place in a warm place to rise.
6 Bake in a hot oven 400°F/200°C (Gas Mark 6) for 30-45 minutes, depending on the size of the cobs or loaves, and allow a shorter baking time for small rolls. Use fresh, or cool and freeze.

Rye and wheat bread

¾ oz (21g) fresh yeast
½ oz (15g) Demerara
sugar
¾ pint (425ml) warm
water

1 lb (455g) wholemeal
flour
8 oz (225g) rye flour
1 teaspoon sea salt

1 Mix the fresh yeast and sugar and dissolve in the warm water.
2 Add half the wholemeal flour to form a very soft dough.
3 Leave this soft dough in a bowl in a warm place, covered with a damp cloth for 20 minutes.
4 Mix the rye flour and remaining wholemeal flour and salt together and add to make into a firm dough with the risen soft dough. Knead very well.
5 Place in a bowl in a warm place, covered, and allow to rise for up to 1 hour.
6 Knead and divide into the desired loaf sizes and place in well-greased tins. Allow to rise again until the loaves are about double in size.
7 Bake at 425°F/220°C (Gas Mark 7) for 30-45 minutes. Cool and use fresh, or freeze.

Sesame rolls

½ oz (15g) vegetable
margarine
1 lb (445g) wholemeal
flour
¼ oz (7g) sea salt
1 teaspoon Demerara
sugar

8 fl oz (225ml) warm
water
¾ oz (20g) fresh yeast
a little milk
½ oz (15g) sesame seeds

1 Rub the margarine into the flour and sea salt.
2 Dissolve the sugar in the warm water and mix the yeast well in; leave to stand in a warm place for 5 minutes.
3 Make into a dough and knead well, leaving the kneaded dough in a warm bowl in a warm place, covered with a damp cloth for ½ hour.
4 Knead the dough again and divide into the size of roll required, moulding into rounds.
5 Brush the rolls with a little milk and dip in sesame seeds.
6 Roll out to secure the seeds and place on warm greased baking sheets; leave to rise in a warm place for ½ hour until well risen.
7 Bake at 425°F/220°C (Gas Mark 7) for 15-20 minutes. Cool and serve fresh; or cool and freeze, wrapped in freezer bags.

Pies and Breads

Wholemeal bread

1 oz (30g) fresh yeast
1½ pints (850ml) warm
  water
3 lb (1.4kg) wholemeal
  flour
1 oz (30g) sea salt

1 Dissolve the yeast in the warm water.
2 Mix the flour and sea salt and make into a dough with the dissolved yeast and water. Knead well.
3 Place in a warm bowl to rise in a warm place, covered with a damp cloth for about 1 hour.
4 Knead the risen dough and divide into the loaf size required.
5 Place in warm greased tins, after kneading the pieces of dough, and allow to rise for up to an hour in a warm place covered with a damp cloth.
6 Bake at 425°F/220°C (Gas Mark 7) for 30-45 minutes. Cool and use; or freeze, as desired.

Wholemeal cobs

2 lb (900g) wholemeal
  flour
¾ oz (20g) sea salt
1 dessertspoon malt
  extract
1 teaspoon molasses
under 1 pint (560ml) warm
  water
1 oz (30g) fresh yeast

1 Mix the flour and salt together.
2 Use a little boiling water to dissolve the malt extrct and molasses then add the warm water and dissolve the yeast in it. Allow to stand for 5 minutes.
3 Make into a dough with the flour and knead well.
4 Allow to rise for up to 1 hour in a covered bowl in a warm place.
5 Knead the dough and divide into 1 lb (455g) cobs; mould these into cob shapes and place on warm greased baking sheets, allowing to rise for up to an hour.
6 Bake at 425°F/220°C (Gas Mark 7) for 30-40 minutes. Cool and use; or freeze, as desired.

Wholemeal bridge rolls

½ oz (15g) vegetable
  margarine
1 lb (455g) wholemeal
  flour
¼ oz (7g) sea salt
½ teaspoon molasses
8 fl oz (225ml) warm
  water
¾ oz (20g) fresh yeast

1 Rub the margarine into the flour and salt.
2 Dissolve the molasses in a little boiling water, then make up to the quantity of warm water; add the yeast, stirring until dissolved.
3 When the yeast starts to ferment a little, mix with the flour and salt into a dough; knead well.
4 Place in a bowl in a warm place, covered, to rise for half an hour.

5 Knead the risen dough and divide into small pieces to make the size of rolls required.
6 Mould the pieces of dough into oblong shapes and place on warm greased baking sheets and leave in a warm place to rise.
7 Brush the tops with a little milk or evaporated milk and bake at 425°F/220°C (Gas Mark 7) for 15-20 minutes. Cool and serve fresh or freeze.

Wholemeal teacakes

½ pint (285ml) warm milk
  and water mixed
1 oz (30g) fresh yeast
1 teaspoon malt extract
4 oz (115g) wholemeal
  flour
2 oz (55g) vegetable
  margarine
1 lb (455g) wholemeal
  flour
½ teaspoon sea salt
½ oz (15g) Muscovado
  sugar

1 Place the warm milk and water, fresh yeast and malt extract into a bowl and whisk until dissolved; add the flour and whisk well in.
2 Leave to stand in a warm place for 20 minutes.
3 Rub the margarine into the flour and salt and make the whole into a dough with the ferment mixture and sugar.
4 Knead the dough and then allow to rise in a warm bowl in a warm place for about 45 minutes.
5 Knead the risen dough and divide into the required number of teacakes. Mould into rounds and leave covered for 5 minutes.
6 Roll out to a teacake size and place on warm greased baking sheets.
7 Allow to rise for 30 minutes and then bake at 425°F/220°C (Gas Mark 7) 20-25 minutes. Allow to cool, then use fresh, or wrap well and freeze.

Date and walnut loaf

8 oz (225g) wholemeal
  self-raising flour
¼ teaspoon mixed spice
1 oz (30g) Muscovado
  sugar
1 oz (30g) chopped
  walnuts
3 oz (85g) chopped dates
2 tablespoons malt extract
2 tablespoons molasses
5 tablespoons milk

1 Mix the flour, spice, sugar, walnuts and dates together.
2 Warm the malt extract and molasses and milk over a low heat and add to the dry ingredients.
3 Mix very well and put into a small size — 1 lb (455g) bread tin.
4 Bake for 1 hour at 325°F/170°C (Gas Mark 3). Cool and use fresh, or freeze, as desired.

Hot cross buns

*just over ¼ pint (150ml)
    milk
1 egg
2 oz (55g) Muscovado
    sugar
¾ oz (20g) fresh yeast
2 oz (55g) vegetable
    margarine*

*1 lb (455g) wholemeal
    flour
1 teaspoon sea salt
1 teaspoon mixed spice
2 oz (55g) currants
2 oz (55g) sultanas*

1 Warm the milk and add to the beaten egg and dissolve the sugar and yeast in the warm liquid. Leave in a warm place for 15 minutes.
2 Rub the margarine into the flour, salt and mixed spice and make into a dough with the liquid, adding the currants and sultanas.
3 Knead and place in a warm bowl slightly sprinkled with flour; cover and leave in a warm place to rise for 1 hour.
4 Knead the dough and divide into 3 oz (85g) pieces, then mould into round or oblong bun shapes, leave to stand for a few minutes and cut a cross onto each of the buns.
5 Place on warm greased baking sheets in a warm position, covered with a damp cloth, to rise for about 30 minutes.
6 Brush the buns over with beaten egg or milk before baking (alternatively you can glaze after baking with sugar dissolved in a little water).
7 Bake at 425°F/220°C (Gas Mark 7) for 15-20 minutes. Cool and use fresh; or wrap and freeze, as desired.

Malt bread

*8 oz (225g) wholemeal
    flour
¼ pint (140ml) warm
    water
2 oz (55g) molasses
3 oz (85g) malt extract*

*1 egg
1 teaspoon baking powder
½ teaspoon bicarbonate of
    soda
3 oz (85g) raisins*

1 Place the flour, water, molasses and malt extract into a bowl and mix together.
2 Put in a warm position for 1 hour.
3 Beat the egg and add the baking powder and bicarbonate of soda, then add the flour mixture together with the raisins. Mix well.
4 Put the mixture into a well-greased 1 lb (455g) loaf tin.
5 Bake at 350°F/180°C (Gas Mark 4) for 1-1½ hours. Remove from the tin when cooked and place on a rack to cool. Use fresh, or wrap and freeze.

10

CAKES AND SCONES

CAKES

From the health point of view it is not wise to eat too many foods containing sugar, even though raw cane sugar is used. I have included several recipes for both large and small cakes, and they do add variety to the daily menu.

It is possible to freeze most cakes, large or small. Freeze them when cool, making sure that they are adequately wrapped, and they will keep for 2-3 months. With sandwich cakes, decorated cakes or buns, freeze plain and add the filling or decoration after defrosting. Defrost large cakes at room temperature for longer than small cakes and place in a hot oven for a few minutes, then cool and serve.

Brazil nut layer cake

6 oz (170g) butter or   4 oz (115g) wholemeal
   vegetable margarine   flour
6 oz (170g) raw cane   4 oz (115g) ground Brazil
   sugar   nuts
3 eggs

1 Cream the butter or margarine and sugar till light.
2 Add the beaten eggs gradually, mixing well into the batter.
3 Carefully fold in the flour and ground nuts then pour the cake batter into a greased and lined tin, smoothing over the top.
4 Bake at 350°F/180°C (Gas Mark 4) for 45-60 minutes.
5 When cool, cut and sandwich with one or two layers of raspberry jam made with raw cane sugar and/or a little whipped cream.

Variation: Use ground walnuts in place of the Brazil nuts to make Walnut Layer Cake.

Almond cake

6 oz (170g) butter or   6 oz (170g) wholemeal
   vegetable margarine   self-raising flour
6 oz (170g) raw cane   4 oz (115g) ground
   sugar   almonds
4 eggs   1 lemon

1 Cream the butter or margarine and sugar till creamy and light.
2 Beat the eggs and add gradually to the creamed mixture, mixing well in.
3 Add the flour and the ground almonds.
4 Finally add the grated lemon rind and sufficient juice to make a soft consistency.
5 Place in cake tin lined with greaseproof paper and bake at 350°F/180°C (Gas mark 4) for 1 hour.

Cake (plain)

8 oz (225g) butter or   natural vanilla essence
   vegetable margarine   10 oz (285g) wholemeal
8 oz (225g) raw cane   flour
   sugar   a little milk if necessary
4 eggs

1 Cream the butter or margarine and sugar till light.
2 Add the beaten eggs gradually, mixing well, then add the flavouring.
3 Carefully fold in the flour, adding a little milk if the mixture is too stiff.
4 Bake in a round or square greased baking tin with a layer of greaseproof paper covering the bottom of the tin.
5 Bake at 375°F/180°C (Gas Mark 5) for 45 minutes to 1 hour.

Marzipan topped cake

6 oz (170g) vegetable
    margarine
6 oz (170g) raw cane
    sugar
3 eggs
natural vanilla essence

8 oz (225g) wholemeal
    flour
raw sugar jam
6 oz (170g) raw sugar
    marzipan
carob or chocolate

1 Cream the margarine and sugar till light.
2 Add the beaten eggs gradually, then add the flavouring.
3 Carefully fold in the flour and divide the mixture between two round sandwich tins lined with greaseproof paper.
4 Bake at 350°F/180°C (Gas Mark 4) for 45 minutes to 1 hour. Cool and freeze at this stage if desired.
5 Sandwich the cakes together with raw sugar jam.
6 Take the marzipan, colour one-third with vegetable chocolate colouring and roll out into a long thin strip.
7 Roll the remaining marzipan into a small round; place the chocolate strip in circles on the round of marzipan, commencing from the centre. Cover with sheet of greaseproof paper and gently roll out the marzipan to the size of the cake.
8 Brush the top of the cake with liquid honey and place the marzipan on top of the cake.
9 Coat the edges or sides of the cake with melted carob bar or chocolate.

Carob cake

6 oz (170g) vegetable
    margarine
6 oz (170g) Muscovado
    sugar
3 eggs
6 oz (170g) wholemeal
    flour

½ teaspoon baking
    powder
1 oz (30g) carob powder
½ teaspoon natural vanilla
    essence
a little milk

1 Cream the margarine and sugar until light.
2 Beat the eggs and gradually add to the margarine and sugar, mixing well.
3 Mix the flour, baking powder and carob powder together and add to the mixture together with the vanilla essence and sufficient milk to give a soft consistency.
4 Line a cake tin with greaseproof paper and pour the cake mix in, smoothing over the top.
5 Bake at 350°F/180°C (Gas Mark 4) for 45 minutes to 1 hour. Cool and serve, or freeze.

Variation: To make Carob Layer Cake add this carob filling.

Filling:
1 oz (30g) vegetable
    margarine
2 oz (55g) Muscovado
    sugar

1 tablespoon carob powder
1 dessertspoon boiling
    water

1 Place all the ingredients in a bowl and mix until light and creamy.
2 Sandwich the cake with this mixture.
3 The top of the cake can be coated in carob, using a carob bar melted in a bowl over hot water with a little margarine — three parts carob bar to one part margarine.

Chocolate or carob cake

3 oz (85g) vegetable
    margarine
6 oz (170g) wholemeal
    flour
1 teaspoon baking powder
½ teaspoon bicarbonate of
    soda
3 oz (85g) Muscovado
    sugar

2 tablespoons chocolate (or
    carob) powder
2 tablespoons molasses
½ teaspoon natural vanilla
    flavouring
¼ pint (140ml) milk (or
    soya milk)

1 Rub the margarine into the flour, baking powder and bicarbonate of soda mixed together.
2 Add the sugar and chocolate powder (or carob powder), together with the molasses, vanilla flavouring and milk to give a soft consistency.
3 Place in a greased cake tin lined at the bottom with greaseproof paper.
4 Bake at 375°F/180°C (Gas Mark 5) for 30-40 minutes. Serve when cool, or freeze.

Cherry and lemon cake

6 oz (170g) butter
6 oz (170g) raw cane
    sugar
3 eggs
8 oz (225g) wholemeal
    flour

1 lemon
2 oz (55g) candied lemon
    peel
2 oz glacé cherries

1 Cream the butter and sugar till quite light.
2 Add the beaten eggs gradually.
3 Add the flour, grated lemon rind, candied peel, glacé cherries and the juice of the lemon.
4 Pour the cake batter into a greased and lined cake tin and bake at 350°F/180°C (Gas Mark 4) for 1-1¼ hours. Cool and serve, or freeze.

Cakes and Scones

Christmas cake

8 oz (225g) butter
8 oz (225g) Barbados
  sugar
4 eggs
8 oz (225g) wholemeal
  flour
2 oz (55g) ground almonds
½ teaspoon cinnamon
½ teaspoon mixed spice

8 oz (225g) raisins
8 oz (225g) sultanas
8 oz (225g) currants
4 oz (115g) mixed candied
  peel
4 oz (115g) glacé cherries,
  chopped

1 Cream the butter and sugar until light.
2 Add the beaten eggs, gradually, mixing well in.
3 Mix the flour, ground almonds, cinnamon and mixed spices together and fold them into the batter.
4 Add the dried fruit, candied peel and glacé cherries.
5 Place into a cake tin double lined with greaseproof paper and bake at 300°F/150°C (Gas Mark 2) for 2 hours, then 275°F/140°C (Gas Mark 1) for a further 2 hours. Cool and keep in a tin or wrap and keep in the freezer until required, defrosting at room temperature, and then finishing the cake with almond paste, and icing if desired. Alternatively, a few blanched almonds can be placed round the cake before baking.

Almond paste

8 oz (225g) ground
  almonds
8 oz (225g) fine raw cane
  sugar

1 egg
a little lemon juice

1 Mix the ground almonds and sugar together; add the egg and lemon juice to mix to a stiff paste.
2 Roll out and cover just the top of the cake, or the top and sides — it might be necessary to make 1½ quantities of the almond paste to do this.
3 Running basket-effect rolling pin over the top of the almond paste makes a very effective finish, and the edges can be made fancy by nipping with the fingers or marzipan nippers.

Coconut cake

4 oz (115g) vegetable
  margarine
4 oz (115g) Muscovado
  sugar
2 eggs

6 oz (170g) wholemeal
  self-raising flour
1½ oz (45g) desiccated
  coconut
2 tablespoons milk

1 Cream the margarine and sugar till light.
2 Beat the eggs and add gradually to the margarine and sugar, mixing well.

3 Add the flour, desiccated coconut and sufficient milk to give a soft consistency.
4 Bake in a tin lined with greaseproof paper at 350°F/180°C (Gas Mark 4) for about 1 hour. Cool and serve, or cool, wrap and freeze.

Dundee cake

6 oz (170g) butter
6 oz (170g) Barbados
  sugar
3 eggs
8 oz (225g) wholemeal
  flour
½ teaspoon baking
  powder

4 oz (115g) raisins
4 oz (115g) sultanas
4 oz (115g) currants
2 oz (55g) candied peel
1 oz (30g) glacé cherries
2 oz (55g) almonds

1 Cream the butter and sugar till light.
2 Add the beaten eggs gradually mixing well in.
3 Fold in the flour and baking powder and all the fruit, mixing very well; add a little milk if the mixture is too stiff.
4 Place into a cake tin lined with greaseproof paper and place the almonds round the top in an attractive pattern.
5 Bake at 325°F/170°C (Gas Mark 3) for 2-2½ hours. Cool and serve, or freeze, as required.

Ginger cake

4 oz (115g) vegetable
  margarine
4 oz (115g) Demerara
  sugar
4 oz (115g) molasses
1 egg

8 oz (225g) wholemeal
  flour
1 teaspoon ground ginger
½ teaspoon bicarbonate of
  soda
2 tablespoons milk

1 Cream the margarine and sugar; add the molasses which has been slightly warmed.
2 Beat the egg and add with the flour and ground ginger.
3 Dissolve the bicarbonate soda in the milk and add to the mixture.
4 Place in a square or round greased cake tin with a piece of greaseproof paper covering the bottom of the tin.
5 Bake at 325°F/170°C (Gas Mark 3) for 1 hour. Cool and serve, or wrap and freeze for future use.

Rich ginger cake

4 oz (115g) butter
4 oz (115g) Demerara
  sugar
8 oz (225g) molasses
2 eggs
8 oz (225g) wholemeal
  flour

1 teaspoon baking powder
1 teaspoon ground ginger
2-4 oz (55-115g) preserved
  ginger (optional)

1 Melt the butter, sugar and molasses.
2 Add the beaten eggs; then fold in the flour, baking powder, ground ginger and preserved ginger cut into small pieces.
3 Add a little milk if the mixture is too stiff.
4 Pour the cake mixture into a baking tin lined with greaseproof paper and bake at 325°F/170°C (Gas Mark 3) for 1-1½ hours. Cool and keep a day or two before using, or wrap and freeze.

Ground rice cake

6 oz (170g) butter or
  vegetable margarine
6 oz (170g) Muscovado
  sugar
3 eggs
6 oz (170g) wholemeal
  flour

3 oz (85g) ground rice
1 teaspoon baking powder
natural vanilla essence
a little milk

1 Cream the fat and sugar till quite light.
2 Gradually add the beaten eggs, mixing well.
3 Fold in the flour, ground rice, baking powder and vanilla essence, mixing carefully together, adding a little milk if necessary.
4 Place in a cake tin lined with greaseproof paper and bake at 350°F/180°C (Gas Mark 4) for 1 hour. Cool and serve, or wrap and freeze.

Ground wheat cake

6 oz (170g) vegetable
  margarine
6 oz (170g) Muscovado
  sugar
3 eggs

natural vanilla essence
4 oz (115g) freshly ground
  wheat
4 oz (115g) wholemeal
  flour

1 Cream the margarine and sugar until light.
2 Gradually add the beaten eggs, mixing them well in.
3 Add the vanilla essence and finally fold in the ground wheat and flour.
4 Place the mixture in a cake tin lined with greaseproof paper and bake 1-1½ hours at 350°F/180°C (Gas Mark 4). Cool and serve, or freeze, well wrapped.

Hazelnut sponge cake

3 eggs
6 oz (170g) Muscovado
  sugar

3 oz (85g) wholemeal flour
3 oz (85g) ground
  hazelnuts

1 Separate the egg yolks and whites and beat the whites until quite stiff.
2 Add the egg yolks and sugar and beat until the mixture is very light.
3 Carefully fold in the flour and ground hazelnuts.
4 Place in a well-greased deep round cake tin, or two sandwich tins.
5 Bake for 40 minutes at 325°F/170°C (Gas Mark 3).
6 When cool, sandwich with raw cane sugar raspberry jam if desired, or freeze, well-wrapped.

Madeira cake

6 oz (170g) vegetable
  margarine
6 oz (170g) Muscovado
  sugar
3 eggs
natural vanilla essence

8 oz (225g) fine wholemeal
  flour
½ teaspoon baking
  powder
1 tablespoon milk

1 Cream the margarine and sugar until light.
2 Add the well-beaten eggs a little at a time, mixing them well in, then add the vanilla essence.
3 Carefully fold in the flour.
4 Dissolve the baking powder in the milk and add, mixing well until the batter is smooth.
5 Place in a tin lined with greaseproof paper and bake at 350°F/180°C (Gas Mark 4) for 1 hour.
6 Allow to stand a minute or two before removing the cake from the tin and place on a cooling rack. When cool, serve, or wrap and freeze.

Cakes and Scones

Nut and banana layer cake

*8 oz (225g) butter or
vegetable margarine
8 oz (225g) raw cane
sugar
4 eggs
6 oz (170g) wholemeal
flour*

*3 oz (85g) ground
hazelnuts
½ teaspoon baking
powder
8 oz (225g) dried bananas
1 large orange
½ teaspoon cinnamon*

1 Cream the fat and sugar until light; add the well-beaten eggs
a little at a time, mixing well in and taking care that the batter
does not curdle.
2 Lightly fold in the flour, ground hazelnuts and baking powder.
3 Place half the cake batter into a greased lined baking tin —
round or square.
4 Put the dried bananas through a mincer and mix with the
orange juice, a little grated orange rind and the cinnamon.
5 Place this mixture on top of the cake batter in the cake tin
and cover with the remaining cake batter, smoothing the top.
6 Bake at 350°F/180°C (Gas Mark 4) for about 1 hour; cool
and serve, or wrap and freeze.

Plain fruit cake

*3 oz (85g) vegetable
margarine
8 oz (225g) wholemeal
self-raising flour
½ teaspoon cinnamon*

*3 oz (85g) raw cane sugar
¼ pint (140ml) pineapple
juice
4 oz (115g) raisins*

1 Rub the margarine into the flour and cinnamon.
2 Dissolve the sugar in the fruit juice and add, together with
the raisins, and mix well.
3 Place the mixture in a well-greased cake tin with greaseproof
paper on the bottom and bake at 350°F/180°C (Gas Mark
4) for 1-1½ hours. Cool and serve, or wrap and freeze.

Note: Orange juice can be used in place of the pineapple juice.

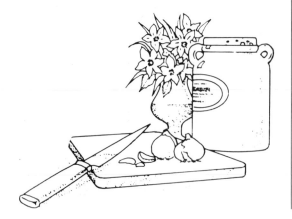

Rice and almond cake

*8 oz (225g) butter or
vegetable margarine
8 oz (225g) Muscovado
sugar
4 eggs*

*4 oz (115g) wholemeal
flour
3 oz (85g) ground rice
3 oz (85g) ground almonds*

1 Cream the fat and sugar until light.
2 Add the well-beaten eggs gradually, mixing well in, taking
care not to curdle the batter.
3 Fold in the flour, ground rice and ground almonds.
4 Place the mixture in a tin lined with greaseproof paper and
bake at 350°F/180°C (Gas Mark 5) for about 1 hour. Remove
from the tin and cool on a cake rack. Serve fresh, or wrap
and freeze.

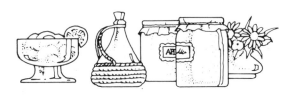

Simnel cake

*6 oz (170g) butter
6 oz (170g) Barbados
sugar
3 eggs
6 oz (170g) wholemeal
flour
1 oz (30g) ground almonds
½ teaspoon mixed spice
½ teaspoon baking
powder*

*6 oz (170g) currants
6 oz (170g) raisins
2 oz (50g) candied peel
1 small lemon
3 oz (85g) ground almonds
3 oz (85g) raw cane sugar
beaten egg*

1 Cream the butter and sugar until light.
2 Add the beaten eggs gradually, mixing well.
3 Fold in the flour, ground almonds, mixed spices and baking
powder.
4 Finally add the currants, raisins, candied peel, grated lemon
rind and juice.
5 Place half the mixture in a tin lined with greaseproof paper
and smooth over.
6 To make the almond paste, mix the ground almonds with the
raw cane sugar and enough beaten egg to make a stiff paste.
7 Roll out the almond paste to the size of the cake tin and place
over the cake mixture.
8 Place the remaining half of the cake mixture on top of the
almond paste and smooth over the top of the cake.
9 Bake in a cool oven 350°F/180°C (Gas Mark 4) for 1 hour,
then lower the temperature to 300°F/150°C (Gas Mark 2)
for 1-1½ hours.

Walnut and raisin cake

8 oz (225g) vegetable
  margarine
8 oz (225g) raw cane
  sugar
4 eggs
a few drops natural
  vanilla flavouring

8 oz (225g) wholemeal
  flour
2 oz (55g) ground walnuts
6 oz (170g) raisins
a little milk
whole walnuts

1 Cream the margarine and sugar until the mixture is light.
2 Beat the eggs and add gradually to the creamed fat and sugar, taking care not to curdle the mixture (this is easier if the eggs are the same temperature as the fat and sugar) and finally add the vanilla flavouring.
3 Fold in the flour, ground walnuts and lastly the raisins and a little milk if the mixture is too stiff.
4 Place in a lined square cake tin and smooth the top over.
5 Place whole walnuts evenly over the top of the cake, spaced so as to make one walnut in the centre of each piece of cake when cut.
6 Bake at 350°F/180°C (Gas Mark 4) for 1-1½ hours.
7 Cool on a rack and cut into square pieces, or wrap and freeze.

Basic wholemeal cake

8 oz (225g) vegetable
  margarine
8 oz (225g) raw cane
  sugar
4 eggs

½ teaspoon natural vanilla
  flavouring
9 oz (240g) wholemeal
  flour
a little milk

1 Cream the margarine and sugar till light.
2 Beat the eggs and add very gradually to the creamed margarine and sugar.
3 When all the egg has been added, add the vanilla flavouring and mix well in.
4 Finally fold in the flour, adding a little milk if the mixture is too stiff.
5 Bake in either a square or round lined cake tin at 350°F/180°C (Gas Mark 4) for about 1 hour.
6 This cake can be served plain, or used to make small decorated cakes, or it can be sandwiched with raw cane sugar jam. Freeze when cool if desired.

Wholemeal butter sponge

2 eggs
3 oz (85g) raw cane sugar
natural vanilla flavouring
3 oz (85g) wholemeal flour

2 oz (55g) vegetable
  margarine, melted
raw cane sugar raspberry
  jam

1 Separate the egg whites and yolks and whisk the whites until quite stiff.
2 Add the egg yolks and sugar and whisk until the whisk leaves ridges when removed from the mixture.
3 Add the vanilla flavouring and carefully fold in the flour.
4 When the flour is nearly mixed in add the melted margarine.
5 Place the cake batter in a well-greased cake tin and bake at 325°F/170°C (Gas Mark 3) for 40 minutes.
6 When cold either wrap and freeze, or cut the cake in two and sandwich with raw cane sugar jam and/or a little whipped cream.

Wholemeal fruit cake

8 oz (225g) vegetable
  margarine
8 oz (225g) Muscovado
  sugar
4 eggs
10 oz (285g) wholemeal
  flour
½ teaspoon ground
  cinnamon

¼ teaspoon ground
  nutmeg
8 oz (225g) raisins
8 oz (225g) sultanas
2 oz (55g) chopped
  candied peel
a little milk or fruit juice

1 Cream the margarine and sugar till quite light.
2 Add the beaten eggs gradually, mixing well.
3 Fold in the flour, ground cinnamon and nutmeg mixed together.
4 Add the remaining ingredients with a little milk or fruit juice if necessary.
5 Pour into a tin lined with greaseproof paper and bake at 325°F/170°C (Gas Mark 3) for 2-2½ hours. Cool on a rack and serve, or wrap and freeze.

Cakes and Scones

Wholemeal sponge layer cake

4 eggs
6 oz (170g) Muscovado
  sugar
natural vanilla flavouring
6 oz (170g) wholemeal
  flour

1 Separate the egg yolks and whites and whisk the whites until stiff.
2 Add the egg yolks and whisk into the whites, together with the sugar. Whisk until the mixture is quite thick; then whisk in the vanilla flavouring.
3 Lightly fold in the flour and place the batter into a deep loose-bottomed cake tin that has been well greased and dusted out with a little flour.
4 Bake at 325°F/170°C (Gas Mark 3) for 1 hour.
5 When cool, cut into four layers and spread the bottom and third layers with raw cane sugar raspberry jam and a layer of whipped cream in the centre. Alternatively, freeze before adding the jam and cream.

Wholemeal sultana cake

6 oz (170g) vegetable
  margarine
12 oz (340g) wholemeal
  flour
6 oz (170g) Demerara
  sugar
1 level teaspoon cinnamon
6 oz (170g) sultanas
2 eggs
½ teaspoon bicarbonate of
  soda
¼ teaspoon cream of
  tartar
2 tablespoons milk

1 Grease and line a square cake tin.
2 Rub the margarine well into the flour.
3 Add the sugar, cinnamon, sultanas and beaten eggs and mix well.
4 Dissolve the bicarbonate of soda and cream of tartar in the milk and add, mixing well in.
5 Place the mixture in the tin and bake at 375°F/190°C (Gas Mark 5) for 1½ hours.
6 Allow to stand a day before cutting, or wrap and freeze.

Wholemeal swiss roll

2 eggs
4 oz (115g) Muscovado
  sugar
3 oz (85g) wholemeal flour
raw cane sugar raspberry
  jam

1 Separate the egg whites and yolks and whisk the whites until stiff, then add the yolks and sugar and whisk well.
2 Carefully fold in the flour.
3 Pour the batter into a Swiss roll tin that has been greased and lined with greaseproof paper.
4 Bake at 400°F/200°C (Gas Mark 6) for 10 minutes.
5 Turn out on to sugared greaseproof paper and, when cooled slightly, spread with raw cane sugar raspberry jam and roll up tightly, using the greaseproof paper to make a nice even roll. Wrap and freeze if desired, or serve the same day.

Almond and raisin buns

4 oz (115g) vegetable
  margarine
4 oz (115g) Muscovado
  sugar
2 eggs
4 oz (115g) wholemeal self-
  raising flour
2 oz (55g) ground almonds
3 oz (85g) raisins

1 Cream the margarine and sugar until quite light.
2 Add the beaten eggs gradually, mixing them well into the creamed mixture.
3 Fold in the flour and ground almonds and lastly add the raisins.
4 Put spoonfuls of the mixture into paper cases in bun tins and bake at 375°F/190°C (Gas Mark 5) for 15-20 minutes. Cool and serve; or pack in freezer bags to store in the freezer.

Almond and raspberry rings

3 oz (85g) vegetable
  margarine
2 oz (55g) Demerara sugar
1 dessertspoon honey
3 oz (85g) wholemeal flour
2 oz (55g) rolled oats
pure almond essence
  (optional)
2 oz (55g) flaked almonds
raspberry jam

1 Lightly cream the margarine, sugar and honey.
2 Add the flour, oats and a little almond flavouring if desired, and mix well. The mixture should be stiff for rolling out.
3 Roll out quite thinly and cut into rounds, then using a small cutter remove the centres from half the rounds.
4 Place the rounds on greased baking trays and sprinkle the hollow rings with flaked almonds.
5 Bake at 350°F/180°C (Gas Mark 4) for 20 minutes.
6 When cool, sandwich together wtih reduced-sugar raspberry jam. Serve fresh, or freeze packed in freezer bags for future use, storing 2-3 months.

Almond crunch

6 oz (170g) butter or vegetable margarine	4 oz (115g) ground almonds
6 oz (170g) Demerara sugar	natural almond flavouring
8 oz (225g) rolled oats	1 small lemon

1 Melt the butter or margarine and sugar over a low heat.
2 Remove from the heat and add the rolled oats, ground almonds, almond flavouring (if desired) and the grated rind and juice of the lemon.
3 Grease a Swiss roll tin and spread the mixture evenly in it, pressing down well.
4 Bake at 325°F/170°C (Gas Mark 3) for 30-40 minutes.
5 Allow to cool for a few minutes before marking the crunch into either square or oblong pieces and when cold remove from the tin. Store in an airtight cake tin. Do not freeze.

Cinnamon oatcake

6 oz (170g) vegetable margarine	2 tablespoons honey
4 oz (115g) Demerara sugar	12 oz (340g) rolled oats
	1 teaspoon ground cinnamon

1 Melt the margarine, sugar and honey.
2 Add the rolled oats and cinnamon and mix well.
3 Grease a Swiss roll tin and place the mixture into it, pressing down well.
4 Bake at 325°F/170°C (Gas Mark 3) for 30 minutes till golden brown.
5 Cool slightly, then cut into squares; remove from the tin when cold and store in an airtight tin. Do not freeze, this cake keeps quite well in a tin.

Chocolate truffle cakes

stale plain wholemeal cake	seedless raw sugar jam
cocoa powder or carob powder	natural vanilla flavouring
	chocolate vermicelli

1 Crumble the stale cake into a bowl. Add sufficient cocoa or carob powder and jam to give the mixture a light chocolate colour and the right consistency to roll into balls. Add a little vanilla flavouring if desired.
2 Roll into balls and then roll the balls in chocolate vermicelli (alternatively desiccated coconut can be used in place of the chocolate vermicelli.)

Coconut oat slices

6 oz (170g) vegetable margarine	1 tablespoon honey
4 oz (115g) Demerara sugar	8 oz (225g) rolled oats
	3 oz (85g) desiccated coconut

1 Place the margarine, sugar and honey in a large pan and gently melt over a low heat.
2 Remove from the heat and add the rolled oats and desiccated coconut.
3 Place the mixture in a greased Swiss roll tin and bake at 325°F/170°C (Gas Mark 3) for about 30 minutes until golden brown.
4 Allow to cool for a few minutes before marking into slices.
5 Remove from the tin when cold and store in an airtight tin. Do not freeze.

Coconut and honey macaroons

2 egg whites	3 oz (85g) desiccated coconut
2 tablespoons honey	natural vanilla flavouring

1 Beat the egg whites till very stiff; add the slightly melted honey and whisk again.
2 Carefully fold in the coconut and vanilla flavouring and place dessertspoonsful of the mixture on to baking tins covered with rice paper.
3 Bake at 350°F/180°C (Gas Mark 4) for 20 minutes, until a light golden brown. Cool and serve. Do not freeze.

Note: Using honey in the macaroons makes them softer. If a crisper effect is desired, substitute the honey with 2 oz (55g) raw cane sugar.

Crunch

8 oz (225g) vegetable margarine	1 tablespoon liquid honey
8 oz (225g) Demerara sugar	12 oz (340g) rolled oats
	natural vanilla flavouring

1 Melt the margarine, sugar and honey in a large pan over a low heat.
2 Add the rolled oats and vanilla flavouring and mix well together.
3 Place the mixture into a well-greased Swiss roll tin and press down well.
4 Bake at 325°F/170°C (Gas mark 3) for 30 minutes until golden brown.
5 Allow to cool for a few minutes and then mark into squares or slices and remove from the tin when cold. Store in an airtight tin. Do not freeze.

Cakes and Scones

Date and honey slices

4 oz (115g) vegetable margarine
3 oz (85g) Muscovado sugar
1 egg
9 oz (225g) wholemeal flour
4 oz (115g) chopped dates
1 tablespoon honey
2 tablespoons pineapple juice

1 Cream the margarine and sugar until light.
2 Gradually add the beaten egg to the creamed mixture.
3 Fold in the flour to make a soft dough.
4 Divide into two and roll into rounds. Place one round in a greased sandwich tin.
5 Mix the chopped dates, honey and pineapple juice together and spread over the mixture in the sandwich tin.
6 Cover with the second round of dough, pressing the edges together.
7 Bake at 400°F/200°C (Gas Mark 6) for 15-20 minutes.
8 Serve hot as a pudding with cream or custard, or cold cut into slices. Freeze when cool if desired, though it will keep for a while in an airtight tin.

Variations:
1 Use minced dried bananas and orange juice with the honey to make Banana and Honey Slices.
2 Use mincemeat to make Mincemeat Slices.

Date rock cakes

8 oz (225g) wholemeal flour
2 teaspoons baking powder
3 oz (85g) vegetable margarine
3 oz (85g) Muscovado sugar
1 egg
3 oz (85g) chopped dates
4 tablespoons pineapple juice

1 Mix the flour and baking powder and rub in the margarine.
2 Dissolve the sugar in the beaten egg and add to the mixture together with the chopped dates and pineapple juice, and mix to a fairly stiff consistency.
3 Place spoonsful on a greased baking tin and bake at 400°F/200°C (Gas Mark 6) for 15-20 minutes. Cool and serve fresh or freeze packed into freezing bags, keeping 2-3 months and defrosting at room temperature. Bake a few minutes in a hot oven to serve crisp and fresh.

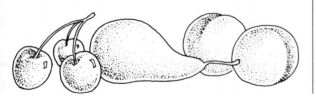

Hazelnut and date buns

4 oz (115g) vegetable margarine
2 oz (55g) Muscovado sugar
1 tablespoon honey
2 eggs
4 oz (115g) wholemeal self-raising flour
2 oz (55g) ground hazelnuts
2 oz (55g) chopped dates

1 Cream the margarine, sugar and honey together until nice and light.
2 Gradually add the beaten eggs, mixing well all the time.
3 Fold in the flour and ground hazelnuts and finally add the chopped dates.
4 Place spoonsful of the mixture in bun tins lined with paper cases.
5 Bake at 375°F/190°C (Gas Mark 5) for 15-20 minutes. Cool and serve; or freeze, packing the buns in freezer bags.

Hazelnut oatcake

8 oz (225g) vegetable margarine
4 oz (115g) Demerara sugar
12 oz (340g) rolled oats
3 oz (85g) ground hazelnuts

1 Melt the margarine; add the sugar, rolled oats and ground hazelnuts.
2 Place the mixture into a greased Swiss roll tin and bake at 325°F/170°C (Gas Mark 3) for 30-40 minutes, until a golden brown.
3 Allow to cool slightly before cutting into squares. Remove from the tin when cold and store in an airtight tin. Do not freeze.

Raisin rock cakes

8 oz (225g) wholemeal flour
2 teaspoons baking powder
3 oz (85g) vegetable margarine
3 oz (85g) Muscovado sugar
1 egg
3 oz (85g) raisins
4 tablespoons milk

1 Mix the flour and baking powder together and rub in the margarine.
2 Dissolve the sugar in the beaten egg and add to the mixture together with the raisins and sufficient milk to make a fairly stiff consistency.
3 Place heaps on a greased baking sheet and bake at 400°F/200°C (Gas Mark 6) for 15-20 minutes.
4 Cool and serve fresh; or freeze, packed in freezer bags for future use.

Muesli buns

4 oz (115g) vegetable margarine	3 oz (85g) unsweetened muesli
4 oz (115g) raw cane sugar	half a lemon
2 eggs	
4 oz (115g) wholemeal self-raising flour	

1 Cream the margarine and sugar until light.
2 Gradually add the beaten eggs, mixing them well into the creamed mixture.
3 Fold in the flour and muesli — if the muesli has any large pieces of nuts in it, chop them into small pieces.
4 Place the bun mixture into paper cases in bun tins and bake at 375°F/190°C (Gas Mark 5) for 15-20 minutes. Serve fresh; or freeze, storing in freezer bags. Makes about 18 buns.

Small sponge cakes

2 eggs	3 oz (85g) wholemeal flour
3 oz (85g) fine raw cane sugar	natural vanilla flavouring

1 Separate the egg whites and yolks and whisk the whites until very stiff.
2 Add the egg yolks and whisk into the whites.
3 Add the sugar and whisk until the whisk leaves peaks in the mixture.
4 Fold in the flour and vanilla flavouring.
5 Place spoonsful of the mixture into paper cases in bun tins.
6 Bake at 400°F/200°C (Gas Mark 6) for 15-20 minutes. Cool and serve plain or make into butterfly buns with a little whipped cream; otherwise, freeze plain and pack in freezer bags to store for future use.

Wheatflake crisp

2 oz (55g) butter	4 oz (115g) wholewheat flakes
1 dessertspoon honey	natural vanilla flavouring
1 oz (30g) Muscovado sugar	

1 Melt the butter, honey and sugar in a pan over a low heat; allow to cook for 5 minutes until quite hot.
2 Remove from the heat and stir in the wholewheat flakes and vanilla flavouring.
3 Place in a well-greased sandwich tin and leave until quite firm in a cool place; cut into pieces and eat while fresh.

Variations:
1 Reduce the quantity of wholewheat flakes by 1 oz (30g) and add either desiccated coconut or ground hazelnuts instead to make Nutty Wheatflake Crisp.
2 Coat the base of the pieces with melted chocolate or carob bar to make Chocolate or Carob Wheatflake Crisp.

SCONES

The method of making any type of scone is easy and takes very little time. Scones make a change from bread or cakes and are delicious served with butter, margarine, peanut butter, jam and so on, either warm or cold. All scones freeze well when cool and can be kept for 2-3 months packed in freezer bags; defrost at room temperature for 1-2 hours and then place in a hot oven for about 5 minutes.

Cheese scones

2 oz (55g) vegetable margarine	2 teaspoons baking powder
8 oz (225g) wholemeal flour	2 oz (55g) grated cheese
	milk to mix

1 Rub the margarine into the flour and baking powder — a little sea salt and freshly ground black pepper can be added if desired.
2 Add the grated cheese and sufficient milk to make into a stiff dough.
3 Roll out and cut into rounds.
4 Place on greased baking sheets and bake 425°F/220°C (Gas Mark 7) for 10-15 minutes. Serve hot or cold, or freeze, as required.

Cakes and Scones

Fruit scones

2 oz (55g) vegetable
   margarine
8 oz (225g) wholemeal
   flour
2 teaspoons baking
   powder
2 oz (55g) Muscovado
   sugar

4 fl oz (115ml) milk
1 oz (30g) sultanas
1 oz (30g) currants
½ oz (15g) candied peel

1 Rub the margarine into the flour and baking powder.
2 Dissolve the sugar in the milk and make into a dough, adding the dried fruit and more milk if necessary.
3 Roll out to the required thickness and cut into rounds.
4 Place on a greased baking sheet and brush with beaten egg or milk.
5 Bake at 425°F/220°C (Gas Mark 7) for 10-15 minutes. Cool and serve, or freeze.

Maize and date scones

2 oz (55g) vegetable
   margarine
4 oz (115g) wholemeal
   flour
4 oz (115g) maize flour
2 teaspoons baking
   powder

2 oz (55g) raw cane sugar
4-5 tablespoons orange
   juice
2 oz (55g) chopped dates

1 Rub the margarine into the flour, maize flour and baking powder.
2 Dissolve the sugar in the orange juice and make into a light dough, adding the chopped dates.
3 Roll out and cut into rounds; place on a greased baking sheet.
4 Brush the tops with a little milk and bake at 425°F/220°C (Gas Mark 7) for 10-15 minutes. Cool and serve, or freeze.

Nut scones

2 oz (55g) vegetable
   margarine
8 oz (225g) wholemeal
   flour
2 teaspoons baking
   powder

2 oz (55g) mixed ground
   nuts
milk to mix

1 Rub the margarine into the flour, baking powder and ground nuts, (one kind of nut rather than mixed nuts, can be used if desired).
2 Make into a dough with sufficient milk.
3 Roll out, cut into rounds and bake on a greased baking sheet for 10-15 minutes. 425°F/220°C (Gas Mark 7). Cool and serve, or freeze.

Oatmeal scones

2 oz (55g) vegetable
   margarine
4 oz (115g) wholemeal
   flour

4 oz (115g) fine oatmeal
2 teaspoons baking
   powder
milk to mix

1 Rub the margarine into the flour, oatmeal and baking powder.
2 Form into a fairly stiff dough with the milk.
3 Roll out, cut into rounds and bake on a greased baking tray at 425°F/220°C (Gas Mark 7) for 10-15 minutes. Cool and serve; or freeze.

Ryemeal scones

4 oz (115g) wholemeal
   flour
4 oz (115g) rye flour
2 teaspoons baking
   powder

2 oz (55g) vegetable
   margarine
1½ oz (45g) Muscovado
   sugar
just under ¼ pint (130ml)
   milk

1 Mix the flours and baking powder and rub the margarine well in.
2 Dissolve the sugar in the milk and make into a dough with the flour.
3 Roll out, cut into rounds and place on a greased baking sheet; brush the scones over with either evaporated milk or beaten egg.
4 Bake at 425°F/220°C (Gas Mark 7) for 10-15 minutes. Cool and serve; or freeze.

Spiced fruit scones

2 oz (55g) vegetable
   margarine
8 oz (225g) wholemeal
   flour
2 teaspoons baking
   powder

½ teaspoon mixed spice
2 oz (55g) raw cane sugar
1 egg
1 dessert apple
2 oz (55g) sultanas

1 Rub the margarine into the flour, baking powder and mixed spice.
2 Dissolve the sugar in the beaten egg, grate the apple and add both to the flour to make into a dough, finally adding the sultanas.
3 Roll out to the desired thickness and cut into rounds; place on a greased baking sheet and brush the top with a little egg or milk.
4 Bake at 425°F/220°C (Gas Mark 7) for 10-15 minutes. Cool and serve, or freeze.

Raisin scones

2 oz (55g) vegetable
    margarine
8 oz (225g) wholemeal
    flour
2 teaspoons baking
    powder

2 oz (55g) Muscovado
    sugar
1 egg
1-2 tablespoons milk
2 oz (55g) raisins

1 Rub the margarine into the flour and baking powder.
2 Dissolve the sugar in the beaten egg and add to the flour together with the milk and raisins to make into a soft dough.
3 Roll out, cut into rounds and place on a greased baking sheet; brush the tops with beaten egg or milk.
4 Bake at 425°F/220°C (Gas Mark 7) for 10-15 minutes. Cool and serve, or freeze.

Note: Replace the raisins with sultanas to make Sultana Scones.

Plain scones

2 oz (55g) vegetable
    margarine
8 oz (225g) wholemeal
    flour
2 teaspoons baking
    powder

2 oz (55g) Muscovado
    sugar
just under ¼ pint (130ml)
    milk

1 Rub the margarine into the flour and baking powder.
2 Dissolve the sugar in the milk and make into a dough.
3 Roll out, cut into rounds and bake at 425°F/220°C (Gas Mark 7) for 10-15 minutes on greased baking sheets. Cool and serve, or freeze.

Variation: Omit the sugar and then the scones can be used in place of bread.

11

BISCUITS AND SWEETS

BISCUITS

It is always useful to have a supply of home-made biscuits in an airtight tin in the store cupboard. There are many recipes for biscuits using only wholefood ingredients and they make a change from cakes and scones. In view of the fact that they can be kept quite well in airtight tins, it is not really necessary to freeze biscuits when made. In the one or two recipes where the biscuit dough is rolled out before the shapes are cut, however, the dough can be wrapped and frozen in an even-shaped roll and kept in the freezer. To use, remove from the freezer and cut the roll into thin slices, place these on a greased baking tray and bake according to the recipe. The biscuit dough will keep 1-3 months.

Almond biscuits

4 oz (115g) butter or
vegetable margarine
8 oz (225g) wholemeal
flour
1 teaspoon baking powder

3 oz (85g) ground almonds
3 oz (85g) raw cane sugar
3 tablespoons pineapple
juice

1 Rub the butter or margarine into the mixed flour and baking powder.
2 Add the ground almonds, sugar and sufficient pineapple juice to form a light dough.
3 Roll out to the desired thickness and cut into rounds.
4 Bake on greased baking sheets at 350°F/180°C (Gas Mark 4) for 15-20 minutes; allow to cool for a few minutes, then place on a rack until they are cold. Store in an airtight tin.

Coconut cookies

4 oz (115g) vegetable
margarine
3 oz (85g) Muscovado
sugar
1 tablespoon honey
4 oz (115g) wholemeal
flour

1 teaspoon baking powder
½ teaspoon bicarbonate of
soda
2 oz (55g) rolled oats
2 oz (55g) desiccated
coconut

1 Cream the margarine, sugar and honey together.
2 Mix all the dry ingredients together and add to the creamed mixture, and mix well.
3 Take small spoonfuls and roll into balls; place on greased baking trays allowing room for the cookies to spread and flatten slightly.
4 Bake at 375°F/190°C (Gas Mark 5) for 10-15 minutes until a nice golden brown.

Digestive biscuits

*8 oz (225g) 100%
  wholemeal flour
4 oz (115g) 81%
  wholemeal flour
1 teaspoon baking powder
3 oz (85g) vegetable
  margarine*

*2 oz (55g) vegetable
  cooking fat
3 oz (85g) Muscovado
  sugar
1 egg
water as necessary*

1 Place both the flours and baking powder into a bowl and rub in the margarine and cooking fat.
2 Add the sugar, beaten egg and just sufficient water to make into a dough.
3 Allow to stand for 15 minutes before rolling out fairly thinly, or alternatively freeze at this stage if desired. Cut into rounds.
4 Place on a greased baking sheet and bake at 350°F/180°C (Gas Mark 4) for 15-20 minutes.
5 Serve plain; alternatively coat the bottom with a little melted chocolate or carob bar, or even fully coat them.

Ginger biscuits

*4 oz (115g) vegetable
  margarine
4 oz (115g) Muscovado
  sugar
1 tablespoon molasses*

*6 oz (170g) wholemeal
  self-raising flour
2 teaspoons ground ginger
1 teaspoon lemon juice*

1 Cream the margarine, sugar and molasses together.
2 Add the flour, ginger and lemon juice and mix thoroughly.
3 Form into small balls, flatten them and place on greased baking trays, allowing room for the biscuits to spread.
4 Bake at 350°F/180°C (Gas Mark 4) for 10-15 minutes.

Hazelnut cookies

*4 oz (115g) vegetable
  margarine
4 oz (115g) Muscovado
  sugar
2 oz (55g) ground
  hazelnuts*

*6 oz (170g) wholemeal
  flour
1 teaspoon baking powder
½ teaspoon bicarbonate of
  soda*

1 Cream the margarine and sugar together.
2 Add the remaining ingredients and mix well together.
3 Take small pieces and roll into balls; place on greased baking sheets, flattening the balls with the hand.
4 Bake at 375°F/190°C (Gas Mark 5) for 10-15 minutes.

Muesli cookies

*4 oz (115g) vegetable
  margarine
4 oz (115g) Muscovado
  sugar
1 dessertspoon honey
4 oz (115g) wholemeal
  flour*

*4 oz (115g) unsweetened
  muesli
1 teaspoon baking powder
½ teaspoon bicarbonate of
  soda*

1 Cream the margarine, sugar and honey together.
2 Add the remaining ingredients and mix well.
3 Divide into small balls the size of a walnut and place on greased baking sheets; flatten the balls slightly.
4 Bake at 375°F/190°F (Gas Mark 5) for 10-15 minutes.

Oat crunchies

*4 oz (115g) vegetable
  margarine
4 oz (115g) Muscovado
  sugar
1 dessertspoon honey
4 oz (115g) wholemeal
  flour*

*4 oz (115g) rolled oats
1 teaspoon baking powder
½ teaspoon bicarbonate of
  soda
½ teaspoon natural vanilla
  flavouring*

1 Cream the margarine, sugar and honey together.
2 Add the remaining ingredients and mix them well together.
3 Take small pieces of the mixture and form into balls.
4 Place on greased baking sheets and flatten them slightly.
5 Bake at 375°F/190°C (Gas Mark 5) for 10-15 minutes.

Variation:
1 Sandwich two Oat Crunchies together with melted carob bar or plain chocolate to make Chocolate Sandwich Crunchies.

Oatcakes

*6 oz (170g) fine oatmeal
2 oz (55g) rice or barley
  flour*

*½ teaspoon sea salt
1½ tablespoons corn oil
boiling water to mix*

1 Mix the oatmeal, flour and sea salt together.
2 Add the corn oil and sufficient boiling water to make into a dough.
3 Roll out to the desired thickness and cut into triangles or rounds.
4 Place on greased baking sheets and bake at 375°F/190°C (Gas Mark 5) for 20-30 minutes. Cool on a wire tray, and serve with butter or margarine and cheese.

Note: Wholemeal flour can replace the rice or barley flour.

Biscuits and Sweets

Oatmeal biscuits

8 oz (225g) wholemeal
  flour
4 oz (115g) fine oatmeal
6 oz (170g) vegetable
  margarine

4 oz (115g) Muscovado
  sugar
1 egg

1 Place the flour and oatmeal in a bowl and rub in the margarine.
2 Dissolve the sugar in the beaten egg and add, mixing lightly into a dough, adding a little water if necessary.
3 Roll out to the desired thickness and cut the biscuits out, or freeze the dough in a neat roll for future use.
4 Place on greased baking sheets and bake at 350°F/180°C (Gas Mark 4) for 15-20 minutes.

Shortbread

9 oz (255g) wholemeal
  flour

3 oz (85g) Muscovado
  sugar
6 oz (170g) butter

1 Mix the flour and sugar together.
2 Add the butter and mix well into the flour and sugar to form a dough.
3 Divide the mixture into two and press into round sandwich tins that have been lined at the bottom with greased greaseproof paper.
4 Bake at 350°F/180°C (Gas Mark 4) for 45 minutes.
5 When cold, cut into pieces.

Variations:
1 Add the grated rind of 1 orange to make Orange Shortbread.
2 Replace 3 oz (85g) wholemeal flour with ground almonds to make Almond Shortbread.

Treacle cookies

8 oz (225g) wholemeal
  flour
½ teaspoon ground ginger
½ teaspoon cinnamon
½ teaspoon bicarbonate of
  soda

4 oz (115g) vegetable
  margarine
4 oz (115g) Barbados
  sugar
1 small egg
2 oz (55g) molasses

1 Mix all the dry ingredients together and rub in the margarine.
2 Add the sugar, beaten egg and molasses and mix well together.
3 Roll into balls the size of a walnut and place on greased baking trays.
4 Bake at 375°F/190°C (Gas Mark 5) for 10-15 minutes.

SWEETS
Occasionally it is nice to have a few home-made sweets, especially to serve on special occasions. The following are just a few ideas, using wholesome ingredients, which are all quite easy to make.

Candy Ice

1 lb (455g) Muscovado
  sugar
¼ pint (140ml) water

4 oz (115g) desiccated
  coconut
4 tablespoons cream

1 Put the sugar and water into a strong pan and dissolve slowly.
2 Boil until it reaches a temperature of 240°F (116°C) and a little of the sugar syrup forms a soft ball when dropped in cold water.
3 Remove from heat and stir in the coconut.
4 Cool for 2 minutes and then add the cream and beat until the mixture thickens; quickly pour into a small well-greased square tin and leave for 5 minutes.
5 Mark into small squares and leave in the tin until cold. Then break into squares, to serve.

Chocolate raisin drops

8 oz (225g) chocolate or
  Kalibu *bar*

6 oz (170g) raisins

1 Melt the chocolate or *Kalibu* bar in a basin over hot water.
2 Add the raisins and mix well.
3 When the mixture thickens a little, drop small spoonsful into paper sweet cases and leave in a cool place until set.

Coconut macaroons

6 oz (170g) chocolate or carob bar
desiccated coconut

1 Melt the chocolate or carob bar in a basin over hot water.
2 Remove from the hot water and stir in sufficient desiccated coconut until the mixture is stiff.
3 Place spoonfuls on greaseproof paper and leave until set then place in small paper sweet cases.

Fruitarian cake

6 oz (170g) dried bananas
6 oz (170g) raisins or sultanas
3 oz (85g) hazelnuts
3 oz (85g) Brazil nuts
rice paper

1 Put the dried fruit and nuts through a mincer and mix well together.
2 Place between two layers of rice paper and press slightly with a rolling pin. Cut into small pieces.

Variations:
1 Use other dried fruits or nuts (e.g. desiccated coconut) and a little grated orange rind and juice can be added.
2 Sandwich the fruitarian cake with raw cane sugar marzipan to give a Marzipan Sandwich fruitarian cake.
3 Sandwich the fruitarian cake with a layer of carob bar or plain chocolate melted and mixed with margarine (3 parts carob or chocolate bar to 1 part margarine) to give Chocolate Sandwich Fruitarian Cake.

Marzipan truffles

4 oz (115g) plain chocolate
1 oz (30g) butter
2 tablespoons evaporated milk
grated rind of 1 lemon
1 tablespoon Muscovado sugar
4 oz (115g) raw sugar marzipan

1 Place the chocolate, butter and evaporated milk in a basin and heat over a pan of hot water for about 15 minutes, stirring until the mixture starts to thicken.
2 Remove from the heat and add the lemon rind and sugar.
3 When cool, form into a long roll.
4 Roll the marzipan out into an oblong shape, the same length as the chocolate roll.
5 Place the chocolate roll on the marzipan and seal its edges round the chocolate roll.
6 Leave in a cool place until quite firm, then cut into slices.

Nutty fruit slices

2 oz (55g) mixed candied peel
2 oz (55g) glacé cherries
6 oz (170g) plain chocolate
1 egg yolk
1 teaspoon cream
½ teaspoon natural vanilla flavouing
2 oz (55g) desiccated coconut

1 Chop the peel and glacé cherries quite small.
2 Melt the chocolate (or use *Kalibu* bar) in a bowl over hot water.
3 Add the egg yolk, cream and vanilla flavouring when the chocolate has melted and beat the mixture until it becomes thick.
4 Stir in the chopped peel and cherries and leave until cool.
5 Take small pieces and form into balls then roll the balls in desiccated coconut.

Snowballs

4 oz (115g) raw sugar marzipan
2 oz (55g) walnuts
1 tablespoon apricot jam
2 oz (55g) desiccated coconut

1 Roll the marzipan out.
2 Chop the walnuts quite finely and sprinkle them over the marzipan then roll up firmly.
3 Take small pieces and form into balls.
4 Coat the balls with the warm apricot jam and roll well in the desiccated coconut.

Index

Index

Index

THE
VEGETARIAN
COOK BOOK 2
More Delicious and Healthy Recipes for All Occasions
DAVID ENO

WITH BARBECUE RECIPES!

Co-published with the Vegetarian Society

THE VEGETARIAN COOK BOOK 2
More Delicious and Healthy Recipes for All Occasions

David Eno shows how the preparation of wholefoods is neither difficult nor time consuming — and the results are delicious enough to tempt the appetite of even the most conservative eater!

An essential guide to cooking and eating natural vegetarian foods, here is all the information you need on wholefood ingredients, their storage and preparation. There are tempting recipes for all occasions, from breakfast through to tea-time and dinner, *including barbecues.* Produced in collaboration with the Vegetarian Society in the same highly successful format as The Vegetarian Cook Book.